Underst

MW00874199

Table of Contents

Introduction

Jap-u, is the first composition in Sri Guru Granth Sahib (SGGS), the Sikh holy book which has the status of the eternal living guru. Jap-u is authored by Guru Nanak (1469 – 1539 CE), the founder of Sikh faith. It is reverently called Japji Sahib or Japji. Mool Mantar or the Root Mantra, which precedes it, is invocation at the beginning of the scripture. Jap-u has a prologue, 38 Paurris/stanzas and a Slok or epilogue. The Sikhs had ten gurus in physical form. However, SGGS contains compositions of the first five and the ninth gurus, along-with saints and bards.

This work is a humble attempt to understand Japji. It is one more English interpretation of Japji but with a different format giving meanings of most individual words in parentheses. It also contains English transliteration of the original at two levels. The first uses the method available on the internet and has been given below the original Gurmukhi. It presents certain difficulties in pronunciation, so an additional transliteration has been given in parentheses in the text. This has been explained in the chapter on Transliteration.

This work endeavours to follow Gurbani Vyaakaran/grammar as worked out by the scholars by looking at Gurbani, the guru. This translation is different from the existing ones at places. It is based on Gurbani grammar, relies less on personal perception and more on what Gurbani says – mostly elsewhere in Japji itself, and in some cases beyond that.

Japji is a complete guide on all aspects of life and contains instructions on how to advance on the spiritual path.

A careful study of Japji shows that Guru Nanak first covers a topic in a Paurri/stanza and elaborates/verifies it in later Paurris.

This feature would be noticed throughout.

Guru Nanak has named this composition as Jap-u. The Sanskrit meaning of Jap is to mutter some word repeatedly. However, contents of Japji are in the form of ਉਪਦੇਸ਼ pronounced Updeysh meaning instruction, to be ever kept in mind and complied with. The Sikh concept of Jap-u therefore is to remember and comply with Naam/Divine virtues and commands. Guru Nanak says about Jap:

ਐਸਾ ਗਿਆਨੁ ਜਪਹੁ ਮਨ ਮੇਰੇ ॥ ਹੋਵਹੁ ਚਾਕਰ ਸਾਚੇ ਕੇਰੇ ॥੧॥ ਰਹਾਉ ॥
Aisā gi▫ān japahu man mere. Hovhu cẖākar sācẖe kere. ||1|| rahā▫o.

*O (**meyrey**) my (**man**) mind, (**japah-u**) remember and put into practice (**aisa = such**) this (**giaan-u = knowledge**) awareness:*
*By which you (**hovhu**) are (**chaakar**) a servant (**keyrey**) of (**saachey**) the Eternal, i.e. you comply with directions of the Creator. 1.*
*(**Rahaau**) dwell on this and contemplate. M: 1, p 728.*

M: 1, p 728 above indicates this verse is by M: 1, the first Guru, given on page 728 of Sri Guru Granth Sahib (SGGS).

Jap means to remember or keep in mind is something known by, or told to, us. It is like keeping in mind directions for travel.

For the sake of clarity, transliteration is in ordinary letters but translation of the text is in italics.

This book contains a number of short essays bringing out themes contained in Japji.

Note on Transliteration

The original content of Sri Guru Granth Sahib is in Punjabi/Gurmukhi script. This book includes transliteration of the original in English at two levels. One is as available on the internet and given immediately below the original Gurmukhi for each line. It has been prepared according to a standard method by scholars.

The internet transliteration presents some problems in pronunciation. It using the same English letter for soft and hard sounds. For example, it uses 't' for both 'ਤ' and 'ਟ'; 'r' for both 'ਰ' and 'ੜ'; or 'd' for both 'ਦ' and 'ਡ'. Punjabi language has two letters namely ਙ and ਞ which are hard to transliterate. It transliteration uses 'ng' for ਙ and Ña for ਞ. However, both these letters start and end with nasal sound.

This book gives a second transliteration in parentheses in the text with translation, for example:

ਆਦਿ ਸਚੁ ਜੁਗਾਦਿ ਸਚੁ ॥ ਹੈ ਭੀ ਸਚੁ ਨਾਨਕ ਹੋਸੀ ਭੀ ਸਚੁ ॥੧॥
Āḏ sacẖ jugāḏ sacẖ. Hai bẖī sacẖ Nānak hosī bẖī sacẖ. ||1||

*The Supreme Being (**sach-u = truth/reality**) existed, and made cosmic laws (**aad-i**) before beginning of creation; has (**sach-u = truth/reality**) existed (**jugaad-i**) from the beginning of ages/time - and through the ages;*
*The Eternal (**hai**) is (**sach-u**) present (**bhi**) even now and (**hosi bhi**) shall also (**sach-u = true**) be present in future, - and so will be Naam/cosmic laws -, says Guru Nanak. 1.*

This work uses 'ngn' for 'ਙ' and 'njn' for 'ਞ'. This fits with the Gurmukhi Alphabet as 'ngn' follows 'g'/'ਗ' and'ਞ' follows 'j'/'ਜ'.

The nasal sound of 'n' like in 'ant' meaning 'end' or limit – not
the insect 'ant' in English - has been indicated with an apostrophe as a'nt.

The internet transliteration also ignores the Lagaa Maatra, i.e. attachments, like the Aunkarr to the last letter in a word like ਤੁ to ਤ and Sihaari ਤਿ to ਤ. These have bearing on translation and meanings. In addition, the internet transliteration does not take the short 'ਰ' as in ਪ੍ਰਭ pronounced Prabh into account and transliterates as Parabh. This work has adopted the following.

Gurmukhi letter	Example of Transliteration	Gurmukhi word
ਉ – u,	utam	ਉਤਮ
ਊ – oo,	ootam	ਊਤਮ
ਓ - o	oh	ਓਹ
ਅ – a	ab	ਅਬ
ਅੰ	a'nn	ਅੰਨ
ਆ – aa	aab	ਆਬ
ਆਂ – aa'n	aa'nn	ਆਂਨ
ਐ - ai	aib	ਐਬ
ਔ - au	oukarr	ਔਕੜ
ਇ – i	ih	ਇਹ
ਈ – ee	eet	ਈਤ
ਸ - s		
ਸ਼ - sh		

ਕ - k

ਖ – kh

ਗ - g

ਘ - gh

ਙ - ngn

ਚ - ch

ਛ - chh

ਜ - j

ਝ – jh

ਞ -njn

ਟ - tt

ਠ – tth

ਡ - dd

ਢ - ddh

ਣ - n

ਤ - t

ਥ – th

ਦ - d

ਧ - dh

ਨ - n

ਪ - p

ਫ - ph

ਬ - b

ਭ - bh

ਮ - m

ਯ - y

ਰ - r

ਲ – l

ਵ – v

ੜ – rr

ਜ਼ - z

ਸ

ਅੰਤ – a’nt, ਅਨੰਤ - ana’nt, ਅਨਤ - anat

ਤਾਂ - taa’n

ਤਾਨ, ਤਾਣ – taan

ਤੇ – tey

ਤਿ where the attachment – Sihaari - to the last letter is silent has been used as ‘raat-i’.
ਰਾਤੀ where the attachment – Bihaari - is not silent has been
given as ‘raati’.

It has not been possible to make distinction between sounds of ‘ਨ’ and ‘ਣ’ and ‘n’ has been used for both.

Synopsis of Japji

Guru Nanak teaches to find the Almighty within, to be at peace. This context facilitates understanding Japji.
Mool Mantar. **Ik Oankaar Sat-i naam-u**. One all-pervasive Supreme Being/Spirit whose Naam-u/writ applies universally. One finds the Almighty with the guru's guidance.
Slok – **Aad-i sach-u**. The Creator existed before the creation came into being and shall ever exist.

Paurris/stanzas with starting words of each.
1. **Sochai soch**. The soul separated from God because of ego remains restless. It tries but cannot find peace though rituals. Success lies in obedience to Hukam/Divine commands or natural laws.

2. **Hukmi hovan aakaar.** Everything happens by Hukam/natural laws, the Sat-i Naam; none is beyond Hukam. One who sheds ego obeys Hukam

3. **Gaavai ko taan.** People praise the Creator's attributes called Kirtam Naam; they ask and the Master keeps giving.

4. **Saacha sahib**. One cannot find God by making offerings or chanting mantras. One obtains human birth based on past deeds. Freedom from births and union with the Almighty comes by Divine grace,.

5. **Thaapiaa na jaaey.** An idol installed by some is not God. The Almighty is self-created/existent. Sing, listen, obey and keep Naam in mind with the guru's guidance.

6. **Teerath naavaa.** Rituals like baths on pilgrimages do not cleanse the mind to find God within. One finds

the Almighty by shedding other methods and obeying Naam. Naam is present within; one obtains its awareness with the guru's guidance.

7. **Jey jug chaarey.** Long life or meritorious acts to impress people do not lead to union with God. It comes with Divine grace, by obedience to Naam.

8-11. **Suniai.** One obtains knowledge and poise by listening to Naam. The devotees then shun transgressions and remain ever happy.

12-15. **Ma'nnai.** Obedience to Naam gives Divine experience; one who obeys alone knows it. This state is beyond description. Obedience shapes the mind and intellect. Obedience to Naam removes impediments to union with the Creator.

16. **Panch parvaan.** Those who obey Naam guided by the guru, are the Panch, the selected ones. They receive recognition here and in the hereafter. They do not try to take measure of the Almighty. God has created creatures of different types with Naam/rules for them are laid down. The creation came into being with one Divine command; the Big Bang theory of the twentieth century is akin to this.

16-19 – The last lines of all three are - **Kudrat-i kavan kahaa veechaar,** i.e. the Creator's powers are awesome. Whatever the Creator decides is best for all.

17. **Asankh jap.** There are people who perform their roles doing what they are meant to do.

18. **Asankh moorakh.** There are those who ignore Naam, act by self-will and commit transgressions. Guru

Nanak says: I, a lowly one am just mentioning this; it is God's play.

19. **Asankh naav.** The creation is vast and diverse with the differing roles and laws/rules applicable. There is none to whom Naam does not apply; none is beyond Divine writ.

20. **Bhareeai hath pair.** The human mind is continuously defiled by watching and hearing evil, thoughts and actions. A person's merits or demerits are known by deeds, not words. Keep away from evil; remember, one reaps what one sows.

21. **Teerath tap daiaa.** Rituals like pilgrimages and charities bring short-lived recognition in the world. Listening to, obeying and keeping Naam in mind, is the inner pilgrimage that purifies the mind. Do not get into arguments about when creation came into being. Only the Creator knows.

22. **Paataala paataal.** Do not try to estimate the number of planets; they are beyond count by the humans, only the Creator knows.

23. **Saalaahi saalaah.** Praise the Almighty and obey humbly such as to be absorbed like the rivers merge in the sea and lose their identity.

24. **Ant na sifti.** Supreme Being is beyond measure. Noone knows Divine plans. Divine writ applies to the highest. Obey Naam to receive Divine grace.

25. **Bahuta karam.** Beneficence of the Almighty is beyond measure; the Divine gives but expects nothing in return. The Almighty knows what is deserved and

gives without asking, but few acknowledge this. One aware of Naam needs nothing more.

26. **Amul gun.** The Almighty is the treasure house of virtues, which the creatures receive and are expected to live by them. Those who do, merge back in the Almighty.

27. **So dar keyha.** Majesty of the Almighty is awesome; the seeker wishes to have vision and asks where does the Almighty live? Answer: The Creator lives in the creation; obey Divine commands and experience Divine presence everywhere.

28-31. **Mundaa santokh.** O Yogi, give up symbolism and lead a productive life. That is the way to unite with the Eternal unchanging Almighty

32. **Ik doo jeebhao.** Ever keep Divine virtues and commands to live by them.

33. **Aakhan jor.** Things like when to take birth and when to die are beyond human strength/capability. These happen as decided by the Divine.

Note: The next four Paurris/stanzas describe five stages of spiritual development

34. **Dharam Khandd:** The realm of Divine/cosmic laws; deeds form the basis of Divine justice.

35. **Giaan Khandd:** The realm of knowledge or awareness and understanding Divine laws.

36. **Saram Khandd:** The realm of endeavour/compliance with Divine laws and transformation.

37, Part 1 – **Karam Khandd**: The realm of Divine grace/enablement.

37, Part 2. – **Sach-u Khandd**: The realm of eternity – union with the Creator.

Paurri 38. **Jat paahaara.** Practice self-control, be free of other ideas and become pure like pure gold. Be imbued with Divine love and mould life by conformance to Divine commands.

Slok (epilogue). **Pavan guru**. Human birth is an opportunity for union with the Creator. Those who conform to Naam in life, succeed.

Japji on Naam

Sikh spirituality is to conform to Naam, i.e. emulation of Divine virtues and obedience of Divine commands, the cosmic laws. In the Sikh arena, therefore, Naam is referred to with reverence. It has two forms Gurbani namely, Divine names/attributes/virtues and writ/Hukam/Divine commands/cosmic laws. An example of the first is:

ਤੇਰੇ ਨਾਮ ਅਨੇਕਾ ਰੂਪ ਅਨੰਤਾ ਕਹਣੁ ਨ ਜਾਹੀ ਤੇਰੇ ਗੁਣ ਕੇਤੇ ॥੧॥ ਰਹਾਉ ॥
Ŧere nām anekā rūp anan̲tā kahaṇ na jāhī t̲ere guṇ ket̲e. ||1|| rahā▫o.

*O Almighty, (**terey**) Your (**naam**) names/attributes are (**aneyka**) numerous and (**roop**) forms (**ananta**) innumerable; it is (**na jaahee**) not possible (**kahan-u**) to say (**key**) how many (**gun**) virtues/attributes You have i.e. they are innumerable. 1. M: 1, p 358. (**Rahaau**) Pause here and reflect.*

The multiple Divine names allude to Divine virtues or attributes. These are Kirtam Naam, i.e. names based on perception of what God does. An example of the second-singular - Naam is:

ਜਿਨੀ ਨਾਮੁ ਧਿਆਇਆ ਗਏ ਮਸਕਤਿ ਘਾਲਿ ॥
Jinī nām d̲hi▫ā▫i▫ā ga▫e maskat̲ gẖāl.

*(**Jini**) those (**dhiaaiaa**) pay attention/conform to (**naam-u**) Naam, they (**gaey**) depart from the world (**ghaal-i**) having put in (**masakat-i**) effort, i.e. acted as directed by the Almighty. Japji Slok/Epilogue.*

The fourth Guru says:

ਜਪਿ ਮਨ ਸਤਿ ਨਾਮੁ ਸਦਾ ਸਤਿ ਨਾਮੁ ॥
Jap man saṯ nām saḏā saṯ nām. M: 4, p 670.

*O (**man = mind**) human being, (**jap-i**) remember and practice (**naam-u**) virtues and commands of (**sat-i**) of the Eternal; (**sadaa**) ever keep in mind, the virtues and commands of the Almighty.*

So Naam Jaap/Simran is of Sat-i Naam-u, the eternal/inevitable commands of the Almighty. Guru Nanak says in Paurri 4 of Japji:

ਅੰਮ੍ਰਿਤ ਵੇਲਾ ਸਚੁ ਨਾਉ ਵਡਿਆਈ ਵੀਚਾਰੁ ॥
Amriṯ velā sacẖ nā▫o vadi▫ā▫ī vīcẖār.

*(**Veechaar-u**) reflect on (**vaddiaaee = greatness**) importance of conformance to (**sach-u**) eternal/inevitable (**naau**) Naam/commands of the Master in (**amrit**) the ambrosial (**veyla = time**) hours of the morning – and conduct yourself by them day and night.*

The fifth Guru puts the two forms of Naam together thus:

ਕਿਰਤਮ ਨਾਮ ਕਥੇ ਤੇਰੇ ਜਿਹਬਾ ॥ ਸਤਿ ਨਾਮੁ ਤੇਰਾ ਪਰਾ ਪੂਰਬਲਾ ॥
Kirtam naam kathey teyrey jihba; satnaam teyra paraa poorblaa. M: 5, p 1083.

The tongue/human being recounts Your names/attributes, o Almighty; but Sat-i naam-u, Your eternal writ/authority has existed from time immemorial - all creation came into being and functions by Sat-i Naam. M: 5, p 1083.

Note: According to Gurbani grammar, in the latter case ਨਾਮੁ Naam-u is singular because the last letter ਮ in ਨਾਮੁ has a line below it. This attachment called Aunkarr indicates a singular masculine entity, among others.

It is hard to understand the meaning of the verse:

ਵਡਾ ਸਾਹਿਬੁ ਊਚਾ ਥਾਉ ॥ ਊਚੇ ਉਪਰਿ ਊਚਾ ਨਾਉ ॥
vadā sāhib ūcẖā thā▫o. Ūcẖe upar ūcẖā nā▫o. Japji Paurri 24.
The available translation on the internet is: "*Great is the Lord and high his seat. His Name is the higher than the high*".

This, particularly the second line, does not seem satisfactory. If however Naam is taken as Hukam, which means rule/writ/command[1], the translation is:

*(**Sahib-u**) the Master is (**vaddaa**) Supreme with (**oochaa**) high/Supreme (**thaau = place**) authority. God's (**naau**) Naam/writ/authority applies (**upar-i**) over (**oochey**) the highest.*

This accords with Paurri 27 saying "So paatsaah-u saah-u paatisahib-u Nanak rahan-u rajaaee" meaning "*The Almighty Supreme Master is the Master of (**paatsaahu**) the Emperors; everyone and everything (**rahan-u**) lives/conforms (**rajaaee**) to ITs will - the Divine writ*".

---

[1] Guru Nanak says: ਏਕੋ ਨਾਮੁ ਹੁਕਮੁ ਹੈ ਨਾਨਕ ਸਤਿਗੁਰਿ ਦੀਆ ਬੁਝਾਇ ਜੀਉ ॥੫॥
"Eyko naam-u hukam-u hai nanak satgur-i deeaa bujhaaey jeeo"
Naam of the Almighty is Hukam; the true guru has given this understanding. M: 1, p 71.

Naam occurs in Mool Mantar and various Paurris of Japji as follows:

Mool Mantar

ੴ ਸਤਿ ਨਾਮੁ

Ik▫oaʼnkār saṯ nām

*(ੴ) pronounced as Ik Oankaar meaning'1' One indivisible, (**oankaar**) Supreme Being whose (**naam-u**) writ/Hukam/authority/rule/cosmic laws are (**sat-i = true**) eternal/inevitable and all encompassing.*

Paurri 4

ਸਾਚਾ ਸਾਹਿਬੁ ਸਾਚੁ ਨਾਇ ਭਾਖਿਆ ਭਾਉ ਅਪਾਰੁ ॥

Sācẖā sāhib sācẖ nā▫e bẖākẖi▫ā bẖā▫o apār.

*(**Saacha**) the Eternal (**sahib-u**) Master whose (**naaey**) Naam/writ is (**saach-u**) eternal, i.e. whose writ ever applies everywhere, is (**bhaakhia = spoken**) praised with (**apaar-u**) infinite (**bhaau**) love by the seekers.*

Note: Guru Nanak asks if making offerings, entreaties and chanting mantras enables to find the Almighty, and says no; the following does.

ਅੰਮ੍ਰਿਤ ਵੇਲਾ ਸਚੁ ਨਾਉ ਵਡਿਆਈ ਵੀਚਾਰੁ ॥

Amriṯ velā sacẖ nā▫o vadi▫ā▫ī vīcẖār.

*(**Veechaar-u**) understand (**vaddiaaee**) greatness/importance of conformance to (**sach-u**) eternal/inevitable (**naau**) Naam/commands of the Master in (**amrit**) the ambrosial (**veyla = time**) hours of the morning – and conduct yourself by them day and night.*

Message: Naam-u is for reflection and compliance.

Paurri 6.

ਮਤਿ ਵਿਚਿ ਰਤਨ ਜਵਾਹਰ ਮਾਣਿਕ ਜੇ ਇਕ ਗੁਰ ਕੀ ਸਿਖ ਸੁਣੀ ॥

Maṯ vicẖ raṯan javāhar māṇik je ik gur kī sikẖ suṇī.

(Ratan, javaahar, maanik* = *precious stones) *wealth of awareness of Naam/Divine virtues and commands - is present* ***(vich-i)*** *in the* ***(mat-i = intellect)*** *human mind, one becomes aware of them -* ***(jey)*** *if one* ***(suni)*** *listens to* ***(sikh)*** *the teachings* ***(ki)*** *of* ***(ik-u = one)*** *the true guru*[1] *– who frees from delusion, to recognize Naam within.*

Message: Naam-u is within; know it with the guru's guidance.

Paurris 12-15

These four Paurris end with:

---

[1] The fourth Guru says:

ਰਤਨੁ ਜਵੇਹਰੁ ਲਾਲੁ ਹਰਿ ਨਾਮਾ ਗੁਰਿ ਕਾਢਿ ਤਲੀ ਦਿਖਲਾਇਆ ॥ ਭਾਗਹੀਣ ਮਨਮੁਖਿ ਨਹੀ ਲੀਆ ਤ੍ਰਿਣ ਓਲੈ ਲਾਖੁ ਛਪਾਇਆ ॥੩॥

Raṯan javehar lāl har nāmā gur kādẖ ṯalī ḏikẖlā▫i▫ā. Bẖāghīṇ manmukẖ nahī lī▫ā ṯariṇ olai lākẖ cẖẖapā▫i▫ā. ||3||

(Gur-i) *the guru* ***(kaaddh-i)*** *brings out from within, i.e. imparts awareness of,* ***(ratan-u = jewel, javeyhar-u = emerald, and laal-u = ruby)*** *the priceless* ***(har-i naama)*** *Divine virtues and commands, and* ***(dikhlaaiaa)*** *shows by placing* ***(tali)*** *on palm of the hand, i.e. imparts awareness of Naam.*

(Manmukh-i = self-willed) *those who do not follow the guru are* ***(bhaag-heen)*** *unfortunate; they do not* ***(leeaa = take)*** *get awareness as* ***(laakkh-u = one hundred thousand)*** *priceless Naam* ***(chhapaaiaa)*** *remains hidden behind* ***(trin = straw)*** *the worthless thoughts of attachments to the world-play. 3. M: 4, p 880.*

ਐਸਾ ਨਾਮੁ ਨਿਰੰਜਨੁ ਹੋਇ ॥ ਜੇ ਕੋ ਮੰਨਿ ਜਾਣੈ ਮਨਿ ਕੋਇ ॥
Aisā nām niranjan ho◌e. Je ko man jāṇai man ko◌e.

*(**Aisa**) such is (**niranjan-u = unstained**) the purifying Naam, (**jey**) if (**ko**) someone (**mann-i**) obeys; but (**koey**) some rare person truly obeys and (**jaanai = knows**) experiences that – freedom from influence of temptations - (**man-i**) in mind.*

Message: Naam-u is for obedience

<u>Paurri 16</u>

ਜੀਅ ਜਾਤਿ ਰੰਗਾ ਕੇ ਨਾਵ ॥ ਸਭਨਾ ਲਿਖਿਆ ਵੁੜੀ ਕਲਾਮ ॥
Jī◌a jāṯ rangā ke nāv. Sabẖnā likẖi◌ā vuṛī kalām.

*There are (**jeea**) creatures (**key**) of numerous (**jaat-i**) types, (**rangaa**) hues and (**naav**) names/attributes/roles. The Creator's (**kalaam**) pen (**vurri**) moved and (**likhiaa = wrote**) allotted roles/made the laws for the role of (**sabhna = all**) each of them.*

Note: (Key Naav) "names of" indicates plural and refers to attributes of creatures.

<u>Paurri 19</u>

ਅਸੰਖ ਨਾਵ ਅਸੰਖ ਥਾਵ ॥
Asaʼnkẖ nāv asaʼnkẖ thāv.

*The Creator has (**asankh**) countless (**naav = names**) attributes and is present at (**asankh**) countless (**thaav**) places, i.e. is all-pervasive.*

ਅਖਰੀ ਨਾਮੁ ਅਖਰੀ ਸਾਲਾਹ ॥
Akẖrī nām akẖrī sālāh.

*The creatures act as the Creator directs; the creatures obey (**naam-u**) Naam/Divine commands (**akhri = by words**) as written on the mind, i.e. motivated from within; they (**saalaah**) praise and emulate Divine virtues when motivated from within.*

ਜੇਤਾ ਕੀਤਾ ਤੇਤਾ ਨਾਉ ॥ ਵਿਣੁ ਨਾਵੈ ਨਾਹੀ ਕੋ ਥਾਉ ॥
Jeṯā kīṯā ṯeṯā nā▫o. viṇ nāvai nāhī ko thā▫o.

*(**Jeyta = as much**) all those (**keetaa**) created (**teyta = that much**) all them have (**naau**) names/roles and commands/cosmic laws applicable, i.e. everyone/thing is subject to Divine laws applicable to them. There is (**naahi ko = not any**) no (**thaau = place**) entity (**vin-u**) without (**naavai**) Naam/Divine law applicable.*

Paurri 20.

ਭਰੀਐ ਮਤਿ ਪਾਪਾ ਕੈ ਸੰਗਿ ॥ ਓਹੁ ਧੋਪੈ ਨਾਵੈ ਕੈ ਰੰਗਿ ॥
Bẖarī▫ai maṯ pāpā kai sang. Oh ḏẖopai nāvai kai rang.

*(**Mat-i**) the mind keeps getting (**bhareeai**) defiled (**kai = of, sang-i = company**) with carnal thoughts and actions. (**Oh-u**) that (**dhopai = washed**) is cleansed (**rang-i = being imbued**) with reminder and obedience (**naavai**) to Naam/Divine commands.*
Message: The mind is purified by practice of Naam rather than by bathing on pilgrimages.[1] .

---

[1] Guru Nanak says:
ਤੀਰਥਿ ਨਾਵਣ ਜਾਉ ਤੀਰਥੁ ਨਾਮੁ ਹੈ ॥ ਤੀਰਥੁ ਸਬਦ ਬੀਚਾਰੁ ਅੰਤਰਿ ਗਿਆਨੁ ਹੈ ॥
Ŧirath nāvaṇ jā▫o ṯirath nām hai. Ŧirath sabaḏ bīcẖār anṯar gi▫ān hai.

*I (**jaau**) go to (**naavan-u**) bathe (**teerth-i**) at places of pilgrimage; that (**teerath-i**) pilgrimage is washing vices off the mind by emulating (**naam-u**) Divine virtues.*

Paurri 21

ਵਡਾ ਸਾਹਿਬੁ ਵਡੀ ਨਾਈ ਕੀਤਾ ਜਾ ਕਾ ਹੋਵੈ ॥

vadā sāhib vadī nā▫ī kīṯā jā kā hovai.

*(**Sahib-u**) the Master is (**vaddaa**) Supreme with (**vaddee**) Supreme (**naaee**) Naam/authority (**ja kaa**) whose (**keetaa**) creation everything (**hovai = happens**) is, i.e. the Creator alone knows.*

Paurri 24

ਵਡਾ ਸਾਹਿਬੁ ਊਚਾ ਥਾਉ ॥ ਊਚੇ ਉਪਰਿ ਊਚਾ ਨਾਉ ॥

Vadā sāhib ūcẖā thā▫o. Ūcẖe upar ūcẖā nā▫o.

*(**Sahib-u**) the Master is (**vaddaa**) Supreme and has (**oochaa**) Supreme (**thaau = place**) authority.*
*God's (**naau**) Naam/writ/authority applies (**upar-i**) over*
*(**oochey**) the highest.*

Paurri 32

ਇਕ ਦੂ ਜੀਭੌ ਲਖ ਹੋਹਿ ਲਖ ਹੋਵਹਿ ਲਖ ਵੀਸ ॥ ਲਖੁ ਲਖੁ ਗੇੜਾ ਆਖੀਅਹਿ ਏਕੁ ਨਾਮੁ ਜਗਦੀਸ ॥ ਏਤੁ ਰਾਹਿ ਪਤਿ ਪਵੜੀਆ ਚੜੀਐ ਹੋਇ ਇਕੀਸ ॥

Ik ḏū jībẖou lakẖ hohi lakẖ hoveh lakẖ vīs. Lakẖ lakẖ geṛā ākẖī▫ahi ek nām jagḏīs. Ėṯ rāhi paṯ pavṛī▫ā cẖaṛī▫ai ho▫e ikīs.

*If (**doo**) from (**ik**) one, the human (**jeebhou**) tongue (**hoh-i**) become a lakh, and from a lakh (**hovah-i**) become (**lakh vees**) twenty lakh; and Naam-u of (**eyk-u**) the One (**jagdees = master of the world**)*

---

*Pilgrimage is (**beechaar-u**) to contemplate (**sabad = Divine Word**) Divine commands and (**hai**) is to get their (**giaan-u**) awareness (**antar-i**) within.*

*the Almighty (**aakheeah-i**) is uttered with every tongue, and emulated by the body.*
*(**Eyt-u**) these are (**pavrreeaa**) the steps of the staircase (**raah-i = the way**) on the path which one needs to (**charreeai**) climb to (**hoey**) become (**ikees**) one/unite (**pat-i**) with, the Creator.*
Message: Naam is for compliance.

Paurri 34

ਤਿਸੁ ਵਿਚਿ ਜੀਅ ਜੁਗਤਿ ਕੇ ਰੰਗ ॥ ਤਿਨ ਕੇ ਨਾਮ ਅਨੇਕ ਅਨੰਤ ॥
Ŧis vicẖ jī▫a jugaṯ ke rang. Ŧin ke nām anek ananṯ.

*There are (**jeea**) creatures of different (**jugat-i = methods**) ways of life and (**rang = colours**) types (**vich-i**) in (**tis-u**) that – the world.*
*(**Tin = them, key = of**) their (**naam**) attributes are (**aneyk**) numerous, (**anant = without end**) beyond count, - with their duties and roles and duties prescribed.*
Note: Naav here is plural and refers to attributes of the creatures.

Slok (Epilogue)

ਜਿਨੀ ਨਾਮੁ ਧਿਆਇਆ ਗਏ ਮਸਕਤਿ ਘਾਲਿ ॥ਨਾਨਕ ਤੇ ਮੁਖ ਉਜਲੇ ਕੇਤੀ ਛੁਟੀ ਨਾਲਿ ॥੧॥
Jinī nām ḏẖi▫ā▫i▫ā ga▫e maskaṯ gẖāl. Nānak ṯe mukẖ ujle keṯī cẖẖutī nāl. ||1||

*(**Jini**) those (**dhiaaiaa**) pay attention/conform to (**naam-u**) Naam, they (**gaey**) depart from the world (**ghaal-i**) having put in (**masakat-i**) effort – as directed by the Almighty.*
*(**Tey**) those (**mukh**) faces are found (**ujley**) clean, i.e. those souls are found without faults and united with the Almighty; (**ketey**) numerous others associated*

*with them (**chhutti** = **freed**) are not detained and also unite, says Guru Nanak. 1.*

Japji and Cosmology

Cosmology is the study of the creation, structure of the universe and the place of the creatures in it. Japji provides considerable information on this. As one progresses in its study, a feeling of being part of the whole universe is experienced. It starts at the individual level and the horizon keeps on widening as one goes through its 38 Paurris/stanzas and the Slok/epilogue.

Initial Slok/prologue.

ਆਦਿ ਸਚੁ ਜੁਗਾਦਿ ਸਚੁ ॥ ਹੈ ਭੀ ਸਚੁ ਨਾਨਕ ਹੋਸੀ ਭੀ ਸਚੁ ॥੧॥

Āḏ sacẖ jugāḏ sacẖ. Hai bẖī sacẖ Nānak hosī bẖī sacẖ. ||1||

The Supreme Being ***(sach-u = truth/reality)*** *existed, and made cosmic laws* ***(aad-i)*** *before beginning of creation; has* ***(sach-u = truth/reality)*** *existed* ***(jugaad-i)*** *from the beginning of ages/time - and through the ages.*
The Eternal ***(hai)*** *is* ***(sach-u)*** *present* ***(bhi)*** *even now and* ***(hosi bhi)*** *shall also be ever present in future, - and so will be Naam/cosmic laws, says Guru Nanak. 1.*

Paurri 2

ਹੁਕਮੀ ਹੋਵਨਿ ਆਕਾਰ ਹੁਕਮੁ ਨ ਕਹਿਆ ਜਾਈ ॥

Hukmī hovan ākār hukam na kahi▫ā jā▫ī.

All ***(aakaar)*** *physical existence* ***(hovan)*** *come into being by* ***(hukam)*** *Divine commands or cosmic laws; it is* ***(na jaee)*** *not possible* ***(kahia)*** *to describe the boundaries of application of Hukam the Creator, i.e. the creation is infinite.*

Paurri 8

ਸੁਣਿਐ ਧਰਤਿ ਧਵਲ ਆਕਾਸ ॥
Suṇi▫ai ḏẖaraṯ ḏẖaval ākās.

*(**Suniai**) by listening to the guru one understands that (**dharat-i**) the earth being held in space and (**dhaval = white bull**) the metaphoric bull supporting it, or (**aakaas**) the sky being like a canopy without support are metaphors for cosmic laws as shown in Paurri 16 below.*

Paurri 16

ਧੌਲੁ ਧਰਮੁ ਦਇਆ ਕਾ ਪੂਤੁ ॥ ਸੰਤੋਖੁ ਥਾਪਿ ਰਖਿਆ ਜਿਨਿ ਸੂਤਿ ॥
Ḏẖoul ḏẖaram ḏa▫i▫ā kā pūṯ. Sanṯokẖ thāp rakẖi▫ā jin sūṯ.

*The metaphoric (**dhoul-u**) white bull represents (**dharam-u**) the cosmic laws, (**poot-u**) son (**ka**) of (**daiaa**) compassion, i.e. the Creator is kind to support the planets in space, by cosmic laws (**jin-i**) which (**rakhiaa**) keep every component of creation (**santokh-u = contented**) obediently (**soot-i = by the thread – like that in a rosary**) in allotted position.*

ਜੇ ਕੋ ਬੁਝੈ ਹੋਵੈ ਸਚਿਆਰੁ ॥ ਧਵਲੈ ਉਪਰਿ ਕੇਤਾ ਭਾਰੁ ॥
Je ko bujẖai hovai sacẖiār. Ḏẖavlai upar keṯā bẖār.

*(**Jey**) if someone (**bujhai**) understands and (**hovai = is, sachiaar-u = is truthful**) knows the truth.*
*Then s/he should tell (**keyta**) how much (**bhaar-u**) load*
*(**dhavlai**) the bull can bear.*

ਧਰਤੀ ਹੋਰੁ ਪਰੈ ਹੋਰੁ ਹੋਰੁ ॥ ਤਿਸ ਤੇ ਭਾਰੁ ਤਲੈ ਕਵਣੁ ਜੋਰੁ ॥
Ḏẖarṯī hor parai hor hor. Ŧis ṯe bẖār ṯalai kavaṇ jor.

*Also, there are (**dharti = earth**) planets (**parai**) beyond (**dharti**) the earth and (**hor-u**) further away from the earth and (**hor-u**) farther away.*
*(**Kavan-u**) what is (**jor-u = strength**) the support (**talai**) under (**tis**) their (**bhaar-u**) load/weight.*

Paurri 19

ਜੇਤਾ ਕੀਤਾ ਤੇਤਾ ਨਾਉ ॥ ਵਿਣੁ ਨਾਵੈ ਨਾਹੀ ਕੋ ਥਾਉ ॥

Jeṯā kīṯā ṯeṯā nā▫o. viṇ nāvai nāhī ko thā▫o.

*(**Jeyta = as much**) as many entities that are (**keetaa**) created (**teyta**) that many are (**naau**) commands/cosmic laws applicable to them.*
*There is (**naahi ko = not any**) no (**thaau**) place (**vin-u**) without (**naavai**) Naam/cosmic laws applicable.*

Paurri 21

ਕਵਣੁ ਸੁ ਵੇਲਾ ਵਖਤੁ ਕਵਣੁ ਕਵਣ ਥਿਤਿ ਕਵਣੁ ਵਾਰੁ ॥ ਕਵਣਿ ਸਿ ਰੁਤੀ ਮਾਹੁ ਕਵਣੁ ਜਿਤੁ ਹੋਆ ਆਕਾਰੁ ॥

Kavaṇ sovelā vakẖaṯ kavaṇ kavaṇ thiṯ kavaṇ vār. Kava ṇ sė ruṯī māhu kavaṇ jiṯ ho▫ā ākār.

Question: *(**Kavan-u**) what was (**su**) that (**veyla = Hindu expression for time, vakhat-u = Muslim expression for time**) time part of the day, what (**thit-i**) day in the lunar cycle and what (**vaar-u**) day of the week.*
*(**Kavan-i**) in which (**ruti**) the season, (**maah-u**) month of the year (**s-i**) it was (**jit-u**) when the creation (**hoaa = happened**) took (**aakaar-u**) form, i.e. came into being?*

ਵੇਲ ਨ ਪਾਈਆ ਪੰਡਤੀ ਜਿ ਹੋਵੈ ਲੇਖੁ ਪੁਰਾਣੁ ॥ ਵਖਤੁ ਨ ਪਾਇਓ ਕਾਦੀਆ ਜਿ ਲਿਖਨਿ

ਲੇਖੁ ਕੁਰਾਣੁ ॥

vel na pā▫ī▫ā pandṯī jė hovai lekẖ purāṇ. vakẖaṯ na pā▫i▫o kāḏī▫ā jė likẖan lekẖ kurāṇ.

Answer: ***(Panddti)*** *the Hindu scholars did not* ***(paaeeaa)*** */find know* ***(veyl/veyla)*** *the time,* ***(j-i)*** *that they could have* ***(keykh-u)*** *written in* ***(puraan-u)*** *a Purana.*
(Kaadeeaa/Kaazis) *The Muslim scholars did not* ***(paaio)*** *find/know* ***(vakht-u)*** *the time* ***(j-i)*** *that could* ***(likhan-i)*** *write* ***(leykh-u = writing)*** *this in* ***(kuraan-u)*** *the Quran.*

ਥਿਤਿ ਵਾਰੁ ਨਾ ਜੋਗੀ ਜਾਣੈ ਰੁਤਿ ਮਾਹੁ ਨਾ ਕੋਈ ॥ ਜਾ ਕਰਤਾ ਸਿਰਠੀ ਕਉ ਸਾਜੇ ਆਪੇ ਜਾਣੈ ਸੋਈ ॥

Thiṯ vār nā jogī jāṇai ruṯ māhu nā ko▫ī. Jā karṯā sirṯẖī ka▫o sāje āpe jāṇai so▫ī.

The Yogi ***(na jaanai)*** *does not know* ***(thit-i)*** *the day of the lunar cycle or* ***(vaar-u)*** *day of the week;* ***(na koee)*** *no one knows* ***(rit-i)*** *the season or* ***(maah-u)*** *the month.*
(Ja) *when* ***(karta)*** *the Creator* ***(saajey)*** *made* ***(sirtthi/srishtti)*** *the universe,* ***(soee = that one)*** *the Creator alone* ***(jaanai)*** *knows.*

Paurri 22.

ਪਾਤਾਲਾ ਪਾਤਾਲ ਲਖ ਆਗਾਸਾ ਆਗਾਸ ॥ ਓੜਕ ਓੜਕ ਭਾਲਿ ਥਕੇ ਵੇਦ ਕਹਨਿ ਇਕ ਵਾਤ ॥

Pāṯālā pāṯāl lakẖ āgāsā āgās. Oṛak oṛak bẖāl thake veḏ kahan
ik vāṯ.

There are lakhs of ***(paataala paataal)*** *lower regions of the earth and lakhs of* ***(aagaasa agaas)*** *skies, i.e.*

there are lakhs of planets with their skies and the lower regions;
*Those (**bhaal-i**) searching for (**orrak**) end/boundary of creation (**oorrak**) ultimately (**thakey**) get tired, i.e. give up, (**veyd**) the Vedas (**kahan-i**) say this with (**ik**) one (**vaat**) voice that efforts to find them do not succeed.*

ਸਹਸ ਅਠਾਰਹ ਕਹਨਿ ਕਤੇਬਾ ਅਸੁਲੂ ਇਕੁ ਧਾਤੁ ॥
Sahas aṯẖārah kahan kaṯebā asulū ik ḏẖāṯ.

(***Kateyba***) *the Semitic scriptures (**kahan-i**) say there are*
*(**atthaarah**) eighteen (**sahas**) thousand planets but their (**asloo**) source is (**ik-u**) One (**dhaat-u**) Creator.*

ਲੇਖਾ ਹੋਇ ਤ ਲਿਖੀਐ ਲੇਖੈ ਹੋਇ ਵਿਣਾਸੁ ॥ ਨਾਨਕ ਵਡਾ ਆਖੀਐ ਆਪੇ ਜਾਣੈ ਆਪੁ ॥ ੨੨॥
Lekẖā ho▫e ṯa likī▫ai lekẖai ho▫e viṇās. Nānak vadā ākẖī▫ai āpe jāṇai āp. ||22||

*However, we can (**likheeay = write**) count only if (**leykha**) count (**hoey**) is possible; but in this case anyone (**leykhai**) counting (**hoey = is, vinaas-u**) dies but the count is not completed.*
*The Creator is (**aakheeai**) is called (**vaddaa**) great because (**aap-u = self**) IT (**aapai**) IT-self (**jaanai**) knows, i.e. about the whole creation, says Guru Nanak. 22.*

Paurri 24.

ਅੰਤੁ ਨ ਜਾਪੈ ਕੀਤਾ ਆਕਾਰੁ ॥ ਅੰਤੁ ਨ ਜਾਪੈ ਪਾਰਾਵਾਰੁ ॥
Anṯ na jāpai kīṯā ākār. Anṯ na jāpai pārāvār.

*(**Ant-u**) extent of (**keeta = made, aakaar-u = physical form**) the creation cannot (**jaapai**) be perceived/seen.*
*There is no (**paaraavaar-u**) near end or far (**ant-u**) end – the creation is infinite - the earth is round and hence without any end.*

<u>Paurri 27.</u> Guru Nanak fascinated by harmony in the whole creation says as follows:

ਸੋ ਦਰੁ ਕੇਹਾ ਸੋ ਘਰੁ ਕੇਹਾ ਜਿਤੁ ਬਹਿ ਸਰਬ ਸਮਾਲੇ ॥

So ḏar kehā so gẖar kehā jiṯ bahi sarab samāle.

*(**Keyha = what type**) which is that (**dar**) gate/approach/seat of authority and (**ghar = house**) place where you (**bah-i**) sit and (**samaaley = take care**) direct all activity and watch, o Creator?*

ਵਾਜੇ ਨਾਦ ਅਨੇਕ ਅਸੰਖਾ ਕੇਤੇ ਵਾਵਣਹਾਰੇ ॥ ਕੇਤੇ ਰਾਗ ਪਰੀ ਸਿਉ ਕਹੀਅਨਿ ਕੇਤੇ

ਗਾਵਣਹਾਰੇ ॥

vāje nāḏ anek asankẖā keṯe vāvaṇhāre. Keṯe rāg parī si▫o kahī▫an keṯe gāvaṇhāre.

*There are (**aneyk asankha**) innumerable (**vaajey**) musical instruments producing different (**naad**) sounds and (**keytey**) numerous (**vaavan-haarey**) players play them in unison.*
*There are (**ketey**) numerous (**gaava-haarey**) singers (**kaheean-i = saying**) singing (**siau**) to (**ketey**) numerous (**raag**) ragas and (**pari = wives of ragas**) raginis/sub-ragas.*

Message: The whole universe functions in harmony by cosmic laws, like components of a musical group obey one director.

Paurri 34

ਰਾਤੀ ਰੁਤੀ ਥਿਤੀ ਵਾਰ ॥ ਪਵਣ ਪਾਣੀ ਅਗਨੀ ਪਾਤਾਲ ॥ ਤਿਸੁ ਵਿਚਿ ਧਰਤੀ ਥਾਪਿ ਰਖੀ ਧਰਮ ਸਾਲ ॥

Rāṯī ruṯī thiṯī vār. Pavaṇ pāṇī agnī pāṯāl. Ŧis vicẖ ḏẖarṯī thāp rakẖī ḏẖaram sāl.

*The Creator created – cosmic laws by which the sun and moon cause – days, (**raati**) nights, (**ruti**) seasons, (**thiti**) phases of the moon, (**vaar**) days of the week. The Creator also created (**pavan**) air, (**paani**) water, (**agni**) fire and (**paataal**) lower regions. (**Vich-i**) in (**tis-u**) that set up, - where everything obeys the cosmic laws -, the Creator has (**thaap-i = installed, rakhee = kept**) placed (**dharti = earth**) the world as (**saal**) place for (**dharam**) performing duties/roles by the creatures.*

ਤਿਸੁ ਵਿਚਿ ਜੀਅ ਜੁਗਤਿ ਕੇ ਰੰਗ ॥ ਤਿਨ ਕੇ ਨਾਮ ਅਨੇਕ ਅਨੰਤ ॥

Ŧis vicẖ jī▫a jugaṯ ke rang. Ŧin ke nām anek ananṯ.

*There are (**jeea**) creatures of different (**jugat-i = methods**) ways of life and (**rang = colors**) types (**vich-i**) in (**tis-u**) that – the world. (**Tin = them, key = of**) their (**naam**) attributes are (**aneyk**) numerous, (**anant = without end**) beyond count, - with their duties and roles and duties prescribed.*

Japji on Karma, Reincarnation and Liberation

Karma is the phenomenon of cause and effect. It literally means 'deeds' and covers thoughts, word and speech. It is based on the principle of 'you shall reap what you sow' and covers both the positive and negative actions and their consequences. Gurbani, the guru's word, often uses the metaphor of the agricultural field to explain this phenomenon. For example:

ਕਰਮ ਧਰਤੀ ਸਰੀਰੁ ਜੁਗ ਅੰਤਰਿ ਜੋ ਬੋਵੈ ਸੋ ਖਾਤਿ ॥ ਕਹੁ ਨਾਨਕ ਭਗਤ ਸੋਹਹਿ ਦਰਵਾਰੇ
ਮਨਮੁਖ ਸਦਾ ਭਵਾਤਿ ॥੫॥੧॥੪॥

Karam d̲harṯī sarīr jug anṯar jo bovai so kẖāṯ. Kaho Nānak bẖagaṯ sohėh d̲arvāre manmukẖ sad̲ā bẖavāṯ. ||5||1||4||

*(**Antar-i**) in this (**jug**) age, (**sareer-u**) the body and its (**karam**) deeds are like an agricultural field; (**jo**) what one (**bovai**) sows (**so**) that (**khaat-i = eats**) reaps.*
*(**Bhagat**) obedient devotees (**sohah-i = look good**) are glorified with union with God, while (**manmukh**) the self-willed persons are denied union and ever (**bhavaat-i**) kept in cycles - of reincarnation. 5. 1. 4. M: 5, p 77.*

Guru Nanak explains this concept thus:

ਮਃ ੧ ॥ ਨਾਨਕੁ ਆਖੈ ਰੇ ਮਨਾ ਸੁਣੀਐ ਸਿਖ ਸਹੀ ॥ ਲੇਖਾ ਰਬੁ ਮੰਗੇਸੀਆ ਬੈਠਾ ਕਢਿ ਵਹੀ ॥

Mėhlā 1. Nānak ākẖai re manā suṇī▫ai sikẖ sahī. Lekẖā rab mangesī▫ā baiṯẖā kadẖ vahī.

*Prologue by the first Guru. (**Aakhai**) says (**nanak-u**) Guru Nanak: (**Rey**) o (**manaa = mind**) human being, (**suneeai**) listen to this (**sahee = correct**) helpful (**sikhiaa = instruction**) guidance. (**Rab-u**) God, (**baittha**) sitting with (**vahee = ledger**) account of deeds (**kaddh-i**) taken out, (**mangeyseea**) shall ask (**leykha**) to account for your deeds, i.e. God, being Omniscient, is aware of all your deeds and shall ask you explain – so be careful.*

ਤਲਬਾ ਪਉਸਨਿ ਆਕੀਆ ਬਾਕੀ ਜਿਨਾ ਰਹੀ ॥ ਅਜਰਾਈਲੁ ਫਰੇਸਤਾ ਹੋਸੀ ਆਇ ਤਈ ॥ ਆਵਣੁ ਜਾਣੁ ਨ ਸੁਝਈ ਭੀੜੀ ਗਲੀ ਫਹੀ ॥ ਕੂੜ ਨਿਖੁਟੇ ਨਾਨਕਾ ਓੜਕਿ ਸਚਿ ਰਹੀ ॥੨॥

Ŧalbā pa▫usan ākī▫ā bākī jinā rahī. Ajrā▫īl farestā hosī ā▫e ṯa▫ī. Āvaṇ jāṇ na sujẖ▫ī bẖīṛī galī fahī. Kūṛ nikẖute nānkā oṛak sacẖ rahī. ||2||

*Names of (**aakeeaa**) transgressors in (**jinaa**) who have (**baaki**) debit balance (**rahi**) left, i.e. who committed acts of commission or omission by not complying with Divine commands (**talba = calls, pausan-i = will be made**) will be called out to present themselves in the Divine court, as accused.*
*(**Ajraaeel-u = Muslim equivalent of Jam, phresta/farishta = angel**) the agent of Divine justice shall (**aaey**) come and (**hosi = shall be**) be present (**taee**) there to take the transgressor in custody.*
*No avenue of (**aavan-u**) coming and (**jaan-u**) going, i.e. for escape, will (**sujhaee**) be available because the soul is (**phahee = trapped**) in (**bheerri**) a narrow (**gali**) lane, i.e. no one can escape Divine scrutiny of deeds.*
*We should remember that (**koorr**) falsehood (**nikhuttai = runs out**) cannot withstand*

*examination; (**orrak-i**) ultimately (**sach-i = truth**) the truthful persons (**rahee**) withstand scuting and are approved for union with God, says Guru Nanak. 2. M: 1, p 953.*

The Guru explains in Asa Di Vaar Paurri 4:

ਅਗੈ ਕਰਣੀ ਕੀਰਤਿ ਵਾਚੀਐ ਬਹਿ ਲੇਖਾ ਕਰਿ ਸਮਝਾਇਆ ॥
Agai karṇī kīraṯ vācẖī▫ai bahi lekẖā kar samjẖā▫i▫ā.

*(**Agai = ahead**) in Divine court, the soul is (**bah-i**) made to sit, i.e. to patiently listen, while its (**karni**) deeds and (**keerat-i**) praise, i.e. positive – as well negative – aspects (**vaacheeai**) are told; (**leykha**) the account (**kar-i**) is made and (**samjhaaia**) explained. M: 1, p 464*

Coverage of Karma in Japji.

Paurri 1.

ਕਿਵ ਸਚਿਆਰਾ ਹੋਈਐ ਕਿਵ ਕੂੜੈ ਤੁਟੈ ਪਾਲਿ ॥ ਹੁਕਮਿ ਰਜਾਈ ਚਲਣਾ ਨਾਨਕ ਲਿਖਿਆ ਨਾਲਿ ॥੧॥
Kiv sacẖi▫ārā ho▫ī▫ai kiv kūrhai ṯutai pāl. Hukam rajā▫ī cẖalṇā Nānak likẖi▫ā nāl. ||1||

Question: *(**Kiv**) how (**paal-i**) the wall of (**koorrai**) of falsehood, i.e. actions which separate the soul from God, (**tuttai**) is broken and one (**hoeeai**) is considered (**sachiaara**) truthful, i.e. there is no impediment to union with the Almighty.*
Answer: *It is (**rajaaee**) by willingly (**chalna = moving**) conducting the self (**hukam-i**) according to Divine commands which came (**likhiaa**) written (**naal-i**) with the soul, i.e. present in the mind; there are rules for every role. 1.*

Paurri 2.

ਹੁਕਮੀ ਉਤਮੁ ਨੀਚੁ ਹੁਕਮਿ ਲਿਖਿ ਦੁਖ ਸੁਖ ਪਾਈਅਹਿ ॥

Hukmī uṯam nīcẖ hukam likẖ ḏukẖ sukẖ pā▫ī▫ah.

*It is (**hukmi**) by Hukam – based on past deeds - that one acts (**utam-u = sublime**) by Naam or (**neech-u = low**) disobeys Naam; this is (**likh-i**) written down and (**hukam-i**) by Hukam/Divine law – of one reaps what one sows - (**dukh**) pain or (**sukh**) comfort/peace (**paaeeah-i**) are accordingly experienced.*

ਇਕਨਾ ਹੁਕਮੀ ਬਖਸੀਸ ਇਕਿ ਹੁਕਮੀ ਸਦਾ ਭਵਾਈਅਹਿ ॥

Iknā hukmī bakẖsīs ik hukmī saḏā bẖavā▫ī▫ah.

*(**Ikna = one type**) some are bestowed (**bakhsees**) grace - are united with the Creator - while (**ikna**) others (**bhavaaeeah-i = caused to wander**) kept in cycles of births and deaths (**sadaa**) forever – they are those who do not comply with Naam.*

Paurri 4

ਕਰਮੀ ਆਵੈ ਕਪੜਾ ਨਦਰੀ ਮੋਖੁ ਦੁਆਰੁ ॥

Karmī āvai kapṛā naḏrī mokẖ ḏu▫ār.

*(**Kaprra = garment – cover for the soul**) a life form (**aavai = comes**) is obtained (**karmi**) based on deeds; (**mokh-u**) emancipation, i.e. liberation from being born, and entry to (**duaar-u = gate**) the Divine abode/union with the Almighty, is obtained (**nadri**) by Divine grace – which is deserved by obedience.*

Paurri 12

ਮੰਨੈ ਜਮ ਕੈ ਸਾਥਿ ਨ ਜਾਇ ॥

Mannai jam kai sāth na jā▫e.

*One who (**ma'nnai**) obeys Naam does not (**jaaey**) go (**saath-i**) with, i.e. is not sent for rebirth by, (**jam**) Divine justice – but honourably unites with the Almighty.*

Paurri 15

ਮੰਨੈ ਪਾਵਹਿ ਮੋਖੁ ਦੁਆਰੁ ॥

Mannai pāvahi mokẖḏuᵒār.

*(**Mannai**) by obedience to Naam, one (**paavah-i**) gets (**mokh-u**) emancipation, i.e. liberation from vices, and entry to (**duaar-u = gate**) the Divine abode/union with the Almighty.*

Paurri 20

ਪੁੰਨੀ ਪਾਪੀ ਆਖਣੁ ਨਾਹਿ ॥ ਕਰਿ ਕਰਿ ਕਰਣਾ ਲਿਖਿ ਲੈ ਜਾਹੁ ॥ ਆਪੇ ਬੀਜਿ ਆਪੇ ਹੀ ਖਾਹੁ ॥ ਨਾਨਕ ਹੁਕਮੀ ਆਵਹੁ ਜਾਹੁ ॥੨੦॥

Punnī pāpī ākẖaṇ nāhi. Kar kar karṇā likẖ lai jāhu. Āpe bīj āpe hī kẖāhu. Nānak hukmī āvhu jāhu. ||20||

*Being (**punni**) virtuous or (**paapi**) a transgressor by God is not by what one (**aakhan-u**) says; it is (**kar-i kar-i karnaa = doing** – thrice) by thoughts, words and deeds – which are (**likh-i**) written and (**lai jaah-u**) taken to the hereafter by the soul.*
*Consequences are imposed based on the principle that what (**aapey = self**) one (**beejai**) sows, (**hi**) only s/he (**aapey**) him/her-self (**khaah-u = eats**) gets.*
*One who transgresses cannot unite with the Almighty, and keeps (**aavh-u = comes**) being born and (**jaah-u = goes**) dying, (**hukmi = by orders**) as Divine-ordained, says Guru Nanak. 20.*

Paurri 25

ਬੰਦਿ ਖਲਾਸੀ ਭਾਣੈ ਹੋਇ ॥ ਹੋਰੁ ਆਖਿ ਨ ਸਕੈ ਕੋਇ ॥

Band khalāsī bhāṇai ho▫e. Hor ākh na sakai ko▫e.

*(**Band-i**) bondage to, and (**khalaasi**) freedom - from being born and experiencing comforts and discomforts – (**hoey**) happens (**bhaanai**) by Divine will; (**na koey = not any**) no one (**hor-u**) else (**sakai**) can (**aakh-i = say**) decide this.*

Paurri 33

ਜੋਰੁ ਨ ਜੁਗਤੀ ਛੁਟੈ ਸੰਸਾਰੁ ॥

Jor na jugṯī cẖẖutai sansār.

*It is not by one's own (**jor-u = strength**) will (**jugti = method**) how (**sansaar-u**) the world (**chhuttai = released**) is given up, i.e. attaining emancipation from rebirth by the self is beyond human capability.*

Paurri 34

ਕਚ ਪਕਾਈ ਓਥੈ ਪਾਇ ॥ ਨਾਨਕ ਗਇਆ ਜਾਪੈ ਜਾਇ ॥੩੪॥

Kacẖ pakā▫ī othai pā▫e. Nānak ga▫i▫ā jāpai jā▫e. ||34||

*It is (**paaey = received**) told (**othai**) there whether one is (**kach**) unbaked – like earthenware - or (**pakaaee**) baked, i.e. whether one has complied with Divine commands or not. It (**jaapai jaaey**) is known on (**gaiaa = going**) getting there, when record of deeds is shown, says Guru Nanak. 34.*

Slok (Epilogue)

ਚੰਗਿਆਈਆ ਬੁਰਿਆਈਆ ਵਾਚੈ ਧਰਮੁ ਹਦੂਰਿ ॥ ਕਰਮੀ ਆਪੋ ਆਪਣੀ ਕੇ ਨੇੜੈ ਕੇ ਦੂਰਿ ॥

Cẖang▫ā▫ī▫ā buri▫ā▫ī▫ā vācẖai ḏẖaram haḏūr. Karmī āpo āpṇī ke neṛai ke ḏūr.

*(**Dharam-u**) Dharam Rai the metaphoric judge of Divine court (**vaachai = says**) narrates (**changiaaeeaa**) merits or obedience and*

*(**buriaaeeaa**) demerits or transgressions - of the creature (**hadoor-i**) before the Almighty.*

*Depending on (**karmi = doings**) deeds (**aapo aapni = own of each**) everyone (**ko**) some – those who conform to Naam – go (**neyrrai**) near/unite with the Almighty while (**ko**) some – the transgressors -, are kept (**door-i**) away.*

Japji on Divine Grace

Wikipedia defines Divine grace thus: Divine grace is a theological term present in many religions. It has been defined as the divine influence, which operates in humans to regenerate and sanctify, to inspire virtuous impulses, and to impart strength to endure trial and resist temptation; and as an individual virtue or excellence of divine origin.

Another definition is “So grace is favour, "unmerited favour." Salvation by Grace. Grace is, therefore, God's unmerited favour - His goodness toward those who have no claim on, nor reason to expect, divine favour.

These take God as a person with supernatural powers. If God was a person, he would not be Omnipresent, Omniscient and Omnipotent. It is reasonable to perceive God as the Spirit or force behind the natural laws by which everything happens. Divine grace is therefore not arbitrary. It must be deserved.

The expressions used in Gurbani for Divine grace are Bakhsees, Nadar-i Karam as a composite expression or Nadar-i and Karam individually. The word Kirpa meaning kindness/mercy is also used.

Note: Nadar is the Punjabi adaptation of the Persian expression ‘Nazar’ or Nazrey karam’ meaning sight of grace.

Divine grace has been covered in Japji as follows:

<u>Mool Mantar</u>

The Almighty is found ਗੁਰ ਪ੍ਰਸਾਦਿ *Gurprasaad-i/with the guru's grace/guidance.*

Paurri 2

ਇਕਨਾ ਹੁਕਮੀ ਬਖਸੀਸ ਇਕਿ ਹੁਕਮੀ ਸਦਾ ਭਵਾਈਅਹਿ ॥

Ikna hukmi bakhsees ik hukmi sadaa bhavaaeeah-i.

It is with Divine directions that some are bestowed grace – for union with the Creator -, while some are caused to be ever in cycles of births and deaths.

And as will be learnt later in Japji Sahib, it is by obeying Divine commands.

Paurri 4

Question: ਫੇਰਿ ਕਿ ਅਗੈ ਰਖੀਐ ਜਿਤੁ ਦਿਸੈ ਦਰਬਾਰੁ ॥ ਮੁਹੌ ਕਿ ਬੋਲਣੁ ਬੋਲੀਐ ਜਿਤੁ ਸੁਣਿ ਧਰੇ ਪਿਆਰੁ ॥

Pheyr k-i agai rakheeai jit disai darbar-u; muhou k-i bolan-u boleeai jit sun-i dharey piaar-u.

What offering we should then make so that the court/presence of Almighty is seen? What word/mantra we should recite hearing which the Almighty bears love/is pleased?

Note: Guru Nanak is asking if making offerings and entreaties helps in finding the Almighty, and says no. The following does.

Answer: ਅੰਮ੍ਰਿਤ ਵੇਲਾ ਸਚੁ ਨਾਉ ਵਡਿਆਈ ਵੀਚਾਰੁ ॥ ਕਰਮੀ ਆਵੈ ਕਪੜਾ ਨਦਰੀ ਮੋਖੁ ਦੁਆਰੁ ॥ ਨਾਨਕ ਏਵੈ ਜਾਣੀਐ ਸਭੁ ਆਪੇ ਸਚਿਆਰੁ ॥੪॥

Amrit veyla sach naau vaddiaaee veechaar-u; Karmi aavai kaprra nadri mokh-u duaar-u; nanak eyvai jaaneeai sabh-u aapey sachiaar-u.

Answer: The Almighty expects nothing material and is not pleased by paeans but by one's conduct, therefore: *(**Veechaar-u**) reflect on (**sach-u**) eternal/inevitable (**naau**) Naam/commands and (**vaddiaaee**) virtues of the Master in (**amrit**) the ambrosial (**veyla = time**) hours of the morning – and conduct yourself by them day and night.*

Paurri 7

ਜੇ ਤਿਸੁ ਨਦਰਿ ਨ ਆਵਈ ਤ ਵਾਤ ਨ ਪੁਛੈ ਕੇ ॥

Je tis nadar na aavaee ta vaat na puchhai key.

*But if grace of the Almighty is not bestowed on him/her, then (**na key**) no one asks of (**vaat = state**) wellbeing, i.e. worldly status does not entitle one to receive honour from the Divine.*

Paurri 15

ਮੰਨੈ ਪਾਵਹਿ ਮੋਖੁ ਦੁਆਰੁ ॥

Mannai paavai mokhduaar-u.

*One who (**mannai**) believes/obeys, is freed of vices and (**Paavah-i**) gets entry to (**duaar-u**) gate to attain union with the Creator and be free from cycles of births and deaths.*

Paurri 16

ਪੰਚ ਪਰਵਾਣ ਪੰਚ ਪਰਧਾਨੁ ॥ ----- ਪੰਚਾ ਕਾ ਗੁਰੁ ਏਕੁ ਧਿਆਨੁ ॥

Panch parvaan; --- Panch ka guru-u eyk-u dhiaan-u.

Panch, those who conform to Naam, are accepted for union with the Almighty; they attain high status ---- they pay single-minded attention to the guru.

Paurri 25

ਬੰਦਿ ਖਲਾਸੀ ਭਾਣੈ ਹੋਇ ॥ ਹੋਰੁ ਆਖਿ ਨ ਸਕੈ ਕੋਇ ॥

Band-i khalaasi bhaanai hoey; hor-u aakh-i na sakai koey.

*Bondage to, and freedom from being born and experiencing comforts and discomforts - happens (**bhaanai**) by Divine will – based on one's deeds. There is no other way.*

Paurri 32

ਸੁਣਿ ਗਲਾ ਆਕਾਸ ਕੀ ਕੀਟਾ ਆਈ ਰੀਸ ॥ ਨਾਨਕ ਨਦਰੀ ਪਾਈਐ ਕੂੜੀ ਕੂੜੈ ਠੀਸ ॥੩੨॥

Suṇ galā ākās kī kītā ā▫ī rīs. Nānak naḏrī pā▫ī▫ai kūṛī kūrhai ṯẖīs. ||32||

*(**Sun-i**) hearing the stories of (**aakaas**) the sky, (**keettaa**) worms – without feathers - also (**aaee = comes**) want (**rees = wishing to copy**) to get there, i.e. hearing of ecstasy Divine experience, those who do not obey Naam also want to have it. They pretend in many ways, but -*
*The Almighty (**paaeeai**) is found (**nadri = with sight of grace**) with Divine grace – Divine approval obtained by complying with Naam; otherwise it is (**koorree**) false (**tthees**) bragging (**koorrai = false**) of a pretender, says Guru Nanak. 32.*

Paurri 33

ਜੋਰੁ ਨ ਜੁਗਤੀ ਛੁਟੈ ਸੰਸਾਰੁ ॥

jor-u na jugti chhuttai sansaar-u.

Acting by *one's own will is not the method by which the world is given up, i.e. emancipation from rebirth, is beyond human capability – it is attained by Divine grace*

Paurri 34

ਤਿਥੈ ਸੋਹਨਿ ਪੰਚ ਪਰਵਾਣੁ ॥ ਨਦਰੀ ਕਰਮਿ ਪਵੈ ਨੀਸਾਣੁ ॥

Tithai sohan panch parvaan; nadri karam-i pavai nessan-u.

*The Almighty accepts those who obey Naam, for union. The sign of acceptance (**pavai = is put**) is marked on them (**nadree**) by Divine grace.*

Paurri 37

ਸਚ ਖੰਡਿ ਵਸੈ ਨਿਰੰਕਾਰੁ ॥ ਕਰਿ ਕਰਿ ਵੇਖੈ ਨਦਰਿ ਨਿਹਾਲ ॥

Sach khandd vasai nirankaar-u; kar-i kar-i veykhai nadar nihaal.

The Formless Supreme Being abides in the realm of the truthful living – and watches and then bestows grace.

Slok/Epilogue

ਚੰਗਿਆਈਆ ਬੁਰਿਆਈਆ ਵਾਚੈ ਧਰਮੁ ਹਦੂਰਿ ॥ ਕਰਮੀ ਆਪੋ ਆਪਣੀ ਕੇ ਨੇੜੈ ਕੇ ਦੂਰਿ ॥

Cẖang▫ā▫ī▫ā buri▫ā▫ī▫ā vācẖai ḏẖaram haḏūr. Karmī āpo āpṇī ke neṛai ke ḏūr.

*(**Dharam-u**) Dharam Rai the metaphoric judge of Divine court (**vaachai = says**) reports (**changiaaeeaa**) merits and (**buriaaeeaa**) demerits of each creature (**hadoor-i**) before the Almighty. Depending on (**karmi = doings**) deeds (**aapo aapnee = own of each**) everyone (**ko**) some – those with virtues –are taken (**neyrrai = near**) the*

*Almighty while (**ko**) some are detained and kept (**door-i**) away.*

Development of thought in Japji

Jap-u reverently called Japji Sahib has 38 Paurris or stanzas and a Slok or epilogue. Jap-u is preceded by an invocation called Mool Mantar or Root mantra/fundamental instruction.

The word Jap-u means to remember or recall and comply.

Jap-u starts with a Slok or prologue, which describes the Almighty existing at the beginning of creation, has been through the ages and shall ever be.

The soul yearns to find the Almighty and this requires unqualified obedience. In Japji, Guru Nanak takes us through the process of doing it. The aim is to deserve Divine grace, which alone can help the soul to unite with the Creator. As will be seen, this is done in light of the real world situations and everyday experiences.

God is present in the mind but is masked by other interests caused by temptations. It is by dispelling the other ideas that God is recognised within

Sequential Paurri/stanza-wise flow of this is as follows; starting words of each Paurri are given to facilitate linkage.

Paurri 1 – Sochai soch. The mind cannot be cleansed of other ideas by washing the body. It cannot be quiet/at peace by remaining silent. Amassing wealth does not bring satisfaction because a craving mind is never satisfied. Clever tricks like pretentious garbs or rituals do not satisfy the conscience and the Almighty; obedience to Divine commands does.

Paurri 2 – Hukmi hovan aakaar. The life form we get comes by Hukam/Divine writ, but no one knows how wide its domain is. Divine commands apply to everyone/everything; none is beyond them. This Paurri also says "Ikna hukmee bakhsees ik hukmi sadaa bhavaaeeah-i" it is by Hukam that some receive Divine grace - and merge with the Almighty. One who does not earn Divine grace, ever remains in cycles of births and deaths. Japji says later many times that Divine grace comes by obedience.

Paurri 3 – Gaavai ko taan. People pray to the Almighty according to their understanding. Some do it to ask for benedictions. Some do it as thanksgiving for having received them, while some praise the Almighty marvelling at Divine majesty. God gives but expects nothing in return.

Paurri 4 – Saacha sahib saach naaey. Naam/Divine commands are inevitable and lovingly given. The creatures ask and the Creator keeps giving. Hearing of and seeing God's benevolence, the seeker wishes to have vision of the giver. The way to attain this is reflecting on Naam/Divine commands first thing in the morning when there are no distractions, and obey them in thought, word and deed throughout the day and night. This Paurri introduces the concept of Nadar or Divine grace and Mokh-u Duaar-u; the latter meaning liberation from attachments to the world-play in life and union with the Creator, thus obviating rebirth.

Paurri 5 – Thaapiaa na jaaey. The Almighty cannot to be installed as an idol and worshipped, but is to be obeyed. One needs to sing/praise, listen to Naam/Divine commands, keep them in mind and obey them with the guru's guidance. Singing, praising and obedience are one composite unit – each one of these even when used alone means all three. This is meaningful because listening is learning which must lead to practice. The guru emphasises that there is only One Creator and provider of all creatures whom we should never forget.

Paurri 6 – Teerath naavaa. God is found by a clean mind, but baths or other rituals do not purify the mind. The mind is purified when by dispelling other ideas. This Paurri cautions that any achievement comes by action not symbolism.

Paurri 7 – Jey jug chaarey aarja. People long life/old age, status, wealth etc. get recognition in the world but these do not help in attaining union with the Divine. This happens by Nadar/sight of grace - Divine grace.

Note: Paurri 5 has prescribed Gaaveeai, suniai, man-i rakheeai bhaau, i.e. sing/praise, listen/lean and obey Naam. Paurri 3 has described singing. Paurris 8-11 below detail the process of suniai/listening and Paurris 12-15 of manneeai/obedience.

Paurris 8-11 all end with the underlying message:

ਨਾਨਕ ਭਗਤਾ ਸਦਾ ਵਿਗਾਸੁ ॥ ਸੁਣਿਐ ਦੂਖ ਪਾਪ ਕਾ ਨਾਸੁ ॥
Nānak bẖagṯā saḏā vigās. Suṇi▫ai ḏūkẖ pāp kā nās.

*The devotees are ever joyful; because (**dookh**) faults and (**paap**) transgressions (**naas-u = destruction**) end (**suniai**) by listening/obeying, as there is no fear of retribution or sense of guilt.*

Paurri 8 - Suniai sidh peer. By listening one gets awareness that the religious guides, whom people revere, owe allegiance to the Almighty. In addition, all creation exists and functions according to cosmic laws.

Paurri 9 – Suniai eesar-u barma. By listening one gets awareness that people worship gods/goddesses, but the latter themselves owe allegiance to the Almighty. Those who ignore the Almighty start praising/obeying when they listen to Naam/virtues of the Almighty.

Paurri 10 – Suniai sat-u santokh-u. Awareness of Naam motivates to live truthfully and be contented, i.e. happily accept Divine will. Listening purifies the mind unlike bathing on pilgrimages; practice of what one listens brings honour like those who read scriptures and follow them; it promotes easy concentration in meditation.

Paurri 11 – Suniai saraa gunaa. By listening, one obtains awareness of hard to obtain virtues. One understands that those in authority are all subject to Divine commands.

Paurris 12-15 all are about obedience to Naam and end with the underlying message:

ਐਸਾ ਨਾਮੁ ਨਿਰੰਜਨੁ ਹੋਇ ॥ ਜੇ ਕੋ ਮੰਨਿ ਜਾਣੈ ਮਨਿ ਕੋਇ ॥
Aisā nām niranjan ho▫e. Je ko man jāṇai man ko▫e.

*(**Aisa**) such is (**niranjan-u = unstained**) the pristine/purifying Naam, only (**jey**) if (**ko**) someone (**mann-i**) obeys; (**koey**) some rare such person (**jaanai = knows**) experiences that freedom from influence of temptations - (**man-i**) by obedience, i.e.*

only one who obeys, knows of this experience perfect peace.

Paurri 12 - Maney ki gat-i. The state of purity and peace of mind, of one who obeys Naam is beyond description. It can only be experienced.

Paurri 13 – Mannai surat-i hovai. One who obeys Naam moulds his/her consciousness, thinking and intellect. S/he acts by Naam under all circumstances and suffers no indignities.

Paurri 14 – Mannai maarag-i tthaak na. One who obeys Naam faces no obstacles on way to union with the Almighty, and unites with honour. S/he does not transgress for being conscious of his/her duties, and focus on the objective.

Paurri 15 – Mannai paavah-i mokh-u duaar-u. Those
who obey Naam attain emancipation – freedom from temptations, leading to peace of mind in life, and union with the Almighty on death and obviation of rebirth.

Paurri 16 Part 1 – Panch parvaan. Paurri 16 has three parts. The first part describes Panch - or selected ones - a term used for those obey Naam and get recognition. They pay single-minded attention to the guru's teachings. The Creator accepts them for union. Paurri 34 elaborated this saying "Tithai sohan panch parvaan" the Panch are accepted and glorified.

Paurri 16 Part 2 – Jey ko kahai karai veechaar-u. This part states expanse of the Creator's creation is beyond estimate. It also states scientific facts, which the scientist discovered much later. For example, it questions the old belief that a bull supports the earth. It says the earth and other planets are held in space according to cosmic laws.

Paurri 16 Part 3 and Paurris 17-19. These Paurris describe the diverse natures of people; some obey God, some are ignorant and act by self-will. Divine writ applies everywhere. All these Paurris marvel at the powers of the Creator. The Almighty has laid down Naam/cosmic laws for each component of the creation. All end with "Vaariaa na jaava eyka vaar; jo tudh bhaavai saaee bbhali kaar; tu sadaa salaamat nirankaar" I adore You, o Eternal Formless Master.

Paurri 20 – Bhareeai hath pair. This Paurri says that in our everyday life, we commit numerous faults, which defile the mind and this dirt can be washed off only by loving obedience of Naam. It also says one does not become good or bad by what one claims to be or is called by the people, but by one's actions. One reaps what one sows, i.e. faces consequences of own deeds.

Paurri 21 Part 1 – Teerath tap daiaa. Purification of the mind comes by obeying Divine commands and thus keeping away from vices. This is Antargat teerath - the inner holy bath.

Paurri 21 Part 2 – kavan s-u veyla. It asks to keep away from the controversy about age of the universe for, no one knows; everyone tries to be wiser than another. Only the Creator knows.

Note: **Paurris 22 to 27** bring out some of the aspects of greatness/majesty of the Creator and vastness of the creation as follows:

Paurri 22 – Paataala paataal. The scriptures of oriental faiths talk of millions of planets while those of

Semitic faiths mention eighteen thousand worlds. No, they are countless and cannot be counted. Only the Creator knows.

Paurri 23 – Saalaahi saalaah. We should praise the praiseworthy Master. A seeker does not try to take measure of the Creator, just humbly obeys and remains absorbed with the Creator like rivers lose their identity on entering the sea.

Paurri 24 – Ant na sifti. The Almighty is Infinite and has no boundary. God's Naam/writ applies to the highest.

Paurri 25 – Bahuta karam likhiaa na. The Almighty is the great benefactor who expects nothing in return for the benedictions given. Everyone asks, some people take and acknowledge, some misuse and forget the Giver. There are some who praise the Master even in in suffering, taking it as a reminder for transgressions. One whom the Almighty bestows understanding of the Divine virtues is the monarch over kings – and need to ask for nothing because this wealth lasts forever.

Paurri 26 Part 1 – Amul gun amul vaapaar. This part describes the soul's journey from leaving the Creator, birth, through life and return to the Creator. It says human beings are like traders whom a businessperson gives funds and sends for business to earn money, i.e. the human beings are expected conduct themselves by Naam. Those who comply remain absorbed in life in, and merge with, the Creator on death.

<u>Paurri 26 Part 2 – Amulo amul-u aakhiaa na jaaey.</u> It

says the Almighty is beyond evaluation/measure and cannot be described. All scriptures, gods, demons acknowledge greatness of the Creator; but the Master's greatness does not depend on who all praise; the Supreme Being is as great as the Supreme Being alone is. There is none to compare with. One should not indulge in frivolous talk on the subject.

<u>Paurri 27 – So dar keyha.</u> Controlling powers of the Creator over the creation are awesome. The vast creation functions as one unit like components of a musical group. O human being, your job is to obey the Supreme Master like the air, water and fire do, what they are meant to do.

<u>Paurris 28-31 – Munda santokh</u>. One of the more vocal religious groups at the time of Guru Nanak were the Yogis, who claimed to attain union with the Creator. The Guru told them they were only engaging in symbolism. He asks them, in these Paurris, to practice what the symbols represent, like contentment, making honest living, paying attention to Divine commands, sharing knowledge and so on. These four Paurris have the common ending "Aadeys tisai aadeys" meaning obeisance/submission to the One Almighty who remains unchanged though ages.

<u>Paurri 32 – Ik du jeebhahu lakh</u>. This Paurri is in preparation for union with the Almighty. It asks the seeker to praise and emulate attributes of the Creator one by one to become like the Master. It describes this process like climbing steps on a staircase and requires effort not just chanting something. It also cautions against aspiring to find God by only imitating the devotees, but not putting in effort.

Paurri 33 – Aakhan jor-u. Union with God requires rising above temptations. This is beyond ਜੋਰੁ (jor-u = strength) ability of the mortals and comes with Divine grace which is received by obedience. This is shown later in Paurri 36.

Note: **Paurris 34 to 37** describe the steps or stages/realms
through which the seeker passes to merge with the Creator.

Paurri 34 – Raati ruti thiti. This is **Dharam Khandd**, the realm of dutifulness – sincerely and instinctively performing duties in the allotted role as human being. One should carry out duties naturally like night/day, seasons, lunar cycles, air, water, and fire act accord with cosmic laws. Everyone's acts are subject to evaluation and in light of their role.

Paurri 35 – Giaan khandd. It is the realm of knowledge/awareness, which says all components of the creation function in unison according to cosmic laws. That is why they are in harmony with one another. Understanding this creates firm commitment to Naam. One who does that, believes whatever God, the Creator, does is for the good of the created and there is none other who can do anything. This keeps transgressions, and hence anxiety away.

Paurri 36 - Saram Khandd. This Paaurri starts with Giaan Khandd mah-i giann parchandd; tihthai naad binod kodd anand-u. This means knowledge/awareness of Naam mentioned in Paurri 35, and its practice, brings happiness, because one keeps vices away and remains anxiety-free. It also shows that Saram Khandd the realm/stage of endeavour follows Giaan Khandd the realm of knowledge/awareness. It says Saram Khandd-u ki baani roop-u. **Saram Khandd** is the realm of endeavour gives good looks, i.e. one transforms/moulds the self. With commitment to Naam, one conforms to it; this transforms one's thinking strengthening the mind to keep temptations and other ideas at bay; and brings it in consonance with Divine commands.

Paurri 37 Part 1 - Karam Khandd ki baani Jor-u. It is the realm of Divine grace. One gets ਜੋਰੁ (jor-u = strength) the ability to overcome temptations/distractions by Divine grace. Then there are no other ideas in mind; one is fully absorbed in the Almighty, happily. One is intimately engrossed in Naam like the yarns in a woven fabric. The devotees experience bliss with God in mind

Paurri 37 Part 2 – Sach khandd-i vasai nirankaar-u. Sach Khandd, the realm of eternity is where the Formless Almighty abides. The Creator is present in all places; every-one/thing moves by Hukam, the Creator is pleased to accept for union, those who reach this state. Those who are united with God, are not reborn. This state is hard to describe.

Paurri 38 – Jat-u paahaara. This final Paurri lists the attributes, which help one remain in the realm of Sach Khandd and emphasises self-control. It may also be seen as covering all the five Khandds.

Slok/Epilogue – Pavan guru. This is the epilogue for the whole of Japji Sahib. It summarises the process of conception, birth, followed by doing duties in accordance with by natural phenomena of day and night. Finally, one's deeds – good and bad, right and wrong – are narrated before God. Based on deeds some come near, i.e. merge, and others remain far – in cycles of births and deaths.

Note: God abides in every living being in his/her conscience. Everything mentioned above about obeying cosmic laws and union with God, refers to acting according to conscience and not being questioned by it. This brings peace of mind.

Avoid Rituals, Comply with Naam

People practise many types of rituals for self-purification. These include sitting quietly in contemplation, Jap/Jaap - muttering a word/mantra, Tap - austerities, penance, pilgrimages, and Sanjam meaning control of senses. These give a sense of satisfaction and bring recognition from people. However, they also generate pride, which negates all efforts for spiritual advancement.

Purification of the mind can only be achieved by clearing it of ego, with awareness of, and compliance with, Divine commands with guidance of the guru. These are present on our conscience, which the guru awakens. This brings peace.

For this his formula is:

ਆਚਾਰਿ ਤੂ ਵੀਚਾਰਿ ਆਪੇ ਹਰਿ ਨਾਮੁ ਸੰਜਮ ਜਪ ਤਪੋ ॥ ਸਖਾ ਸੈਨੁ ਪਿਆਰੁ ਪ੍ਰੀਤਮੁ ਨਾਮੁ ਹਰਿ ਕਾ ਜਪੁ ਜਪੋ ॥੨॥

Ācẖār ṯū vīcẖār āpe har nām sanjam jap ṯapo. Sakẖā sain pi▫ār parīṯam nām har kā jap japo. ||2||

*If (**too**) you (**veechaar-i**) reflect it would be realized that (**aacchaar-i = way of living**) living by (**naam-u**) commands of (**har-i**) the Almighty is more satisfying than rituals of (**sanjam**) control of the senses, (**jap**) chanting mantras or practicing (**tapo**) austerities – living as ascetics.*

*Therefore (**japo**) remember and obey (**naam-u**) Naam/commands (**ka**) of (**har-i**) the Almighty; that is what (**jap-u**) needs to be remembered; make Naam your (**sakhaa**) friend and (**sain**) relative/companion; this is (**piaar-u**) love of (**preetam**) the Beloved Almighty. 2. M: 1, p 1113.*

Significantly, Jap-u – meaning remember and comply – is the first composition in the Sikh scripture Sri Guru Granth Sahib. It comprises of a Slok/prologue, 38 Paurris or stanzas and a Slok/epilogue. It is the guide for a practical life. Guru Nanak says elsewhere:

ਐਸਾ ਗਿਆਨੁ ਜਪਹੁ ਮਨ ਮੇਰੇ ॥ ਹੋਵਹੁ ਚਾਕਰ ਸਾਚੇ ਕੇਰੇ ॥੧॥ ਰਹਾਉ ॥

Aisā gi▫ān japahu man mere. Hovhu cẖākar sācẖe kere. ||1|| rahā▫o.

*O (**meyrey**) my (**man**) mind, (**japahu**) remember and put into practice (**giaan-u = knowledge**) awareness – Divine commands present within - (**aisa = such**) thus:*

*(**Hovhu**) be (**chaakar**) servants (**keyrey**) of (**saachey**) the Eternal, i.e. comply with directions of the Creator. 1.*

*(**Rahaau**) dwell on this and contemplate. M: 1, p 728.*

This is how a life of action is emphasised throughout Japji.

Paurri 1

Question: What is the way to find God? *Answer:* Comply with Hukam/Naam/Divine commands willingly.

Paurri 2

Hukam/Divine writ applies to all, no one is beyond it. One who understands this, does not neglect Divine commands and talk/act by ego/self-will.

Paurri 3

(Hukmi = order-giver) the Almighty shows the path/motivates from within and one should comply with Divine commands.

Paurri 4

Reflect on Naam in early morning when distractions are minimal. Union with the Almighty - thus obviating rebirth – comes with obedience to Naam.

Paurri 5

One who serves/obeys the Almighty, receives honour. The way to do it is to praise/acknowledge, listen and act with Naam in mind.

Paurri 6

Nothing is achieved without action or obedience; God is not found by ritual baths as they do not purify the mind – obedience guided by the guru, does.

Paurri 7

Long life and worldly status bring recognition from the people, but do not aid acceptance by the Almighty. It comes by Divine grace deserved by obedience.

Paurris 8-11

Listen/pay attention to Naam; it keeps one away from transgressions and anxiety. One who listens and complies remains ever happy.

Purris 12-15

Comply with Naam. The state of purification obtained by obedience can only be experienced and is beyond description. It removes all obstacles on the path to emancipation – freedom from temptations in life and union with the Creator, thus obviating rebirth after death.

Paurri 16

Panch are those who live in obedience to Naam/Divine commands, and receive acceptance for union with God. All components of the universe exist and function according to cosmic laws and creatures should obey the laws applicable to them.

Paurri 19

Everyone/everything created has Naam/natural laws applicable; there is no place where Naam does not apply.

Paurri 20

Evil thoughts, company and actions in daily life defile the human mind. Obedience to Naam cleanses it. The law "as one sows, so one reaps" applies to all.

Paurri 21

Re-emphasises the Paurri 5 prescription to listen, comply and keep Naam in mind. Devotion/obedience does not develop without awareness of Divine attributes.

Paurri 24

It says: Oochey oopar-i oochaa naau" Naam/Divine writ/cosmic laws are supreme, and apply to the highest and must be obeyed.

Paurri 27

All components of the universe exist in harmony by complying with cosmic laws. The Almighty is the Emperor over kings; everyone is subject to Divine commands/cosmic laws.

Paurri 32

Acknowledging, emulating virtues, and obeying commands of, the Almighty is the figurative climbing steps of the staircase leading to union with the Creator. Union with the Almighty is attained by Divine grace, the pretenders only brag.

Paurris 34-37

These Paurris describe the five realms or steps leading to the Almighty.

Paurri 34. Dharam Khandd – the realm of dutifulness, realising one's duties in the role as human being. Everyone is judged by deeds.

Paurri 35. Giaan khandd – the realm of knowledge, understanding that everyone/everything created complies with Divine commands, and so should the human beings.

Paurri 36. Saram Khandd – the realm of endeavour. Giaan Khandd/awareness of Naam - preceding this state enables to overcome temptations and brings great joy. One then fashions one's life to accord with Naam.

Paurri 37 part 1, Karam Khandd – the realm of grace. One deserves Divine grace by obedience to Divine commands. In this state, the mind has only the Almighty in mind. The devotees enjoy this state as they are not troubled by other ideas.

Paurri 37 part 2 – Sach Khandd, the realm of truth/eternity. This is where the soul having overcome temptations, enters abode of, i.e. unites with, the

Formless Master. This is the state of total compliance with Hukam/Divine commands/cosmic laws.

Paurri 38

Lead a life of purity with discipline and loving obedience to God.

Slok/Epilogue

God metaphorically considers Good and bad deeds of the creatures. As a result, some merge with the Almighty, while some are kept away – the latter remain in cycles of births and deaths. Those who remember Naam, carry out the duties assigned to them and attain union with the Creator.

Paurri-Wise Interpretation of Japji

Mool Mantar.

Jap-u, reverently called Japji Sahib or Japji is the first composition in Sri Guru Granth Sahib (SGGS) also called Gurbani – the gurus' words. Its author is Guru Nanak, the first Sikh guru and founder of the faith. It is preceded by an invocation called the Mool Mantar or the Root Mantra, which is not part of Jap-u but a prologue for the whole of SGGS. It is repeated in full, or abbreviated forms, throughout the scripture. It describes the Divine thus:

ੴ ਸਤਿ ਨਾਮੁ ਕਰਤਾ ਪੁਰਖੁ ਨਿਰਭਉ ਨਿਰਵੈਰੁ ਅਕਾਲ ਮੂਰਤਿ ਅਜੂਨੀ ਸੈਭੰ ਗੁਰ ਪ੍ਰਸਾਦਿ ॥

Ik▫oaʼnkār sat̤ nām kart̤ā purakẖ nirbẖa▫o nirvair akāl mūrat̤ ajūnī saibẖaʼn gur parsāḏ.

I – Traditional Meaning:

The Mool Mantar has two parts.

*(ੴ) pronounced as Ik Oankaar meaning'1' One indivisible, (**oankaar**) Supreme Being whose (**naam-u**) writ/Hukam/authority/rule/cosmic laws are (**sat-i = true**) eternal/inevitable and all encompassing.*
*The Supreme Being is (**karta**) the Creator, (**purakh-u**) all pervasive, (**nir-bhau = without fear**) - does not favour any one, (**nir-vair-u = without enmity**) holds nothing against any one, (**akaal = timeless/deathless, moorat-i = picture/embodiment of**) is Eternal, (**ajooni**) unborn; (**saibha'n**) self-created/existent; is found/known (**gur = guru, prasaad-i = with grace of**) with the Guru's grace/guidance.*

The above meaning is the devotee's perception of a Formless authority also referred to as Jot/Jyoti meaning Light or the Spirit by which all creation was created, exists and functions. It is the foundation of Sikh faith. It may be understood thus:

੧. Numeral '1'. It has three connotations.

- Unique.
- Indivisible.
- Beginning – itself the beginning, without a source, like there is nothing before the numeral '1'.

ੴ Ik Oankaar. This sounds like 'Omkar' of Hindu belief where 'Om' is written as AUM, alluding to the Supreme Being with its three letters representing the Hindu trinity of Brahma – the creator, Vishnu – the sustainer and Mahesh/Shiva – the destroyer. However, use of the numeral '1' before Oankaar discounts that interpretation because the numeral '1' is indivisible. Oankaar occurs in Gurbani for the Almighty e.g. Oankaar brahma utpat-i, M: 1, p 929, meaning *Oankaar created Brahma* who is considered the Creator in Hindu belief. This shows 1 Oankaar does not represent the Hindu trinity. ੴ is therefore to be taken as a single indivisible representation of the Supreme Being. While the numeral 1 has been explained above Oankaar represents the physical creation with 'kaar' or 'aakaar' meaning form or shape. So Ik Oankaar means Creator and the whole creation is manifestation of the Creator, who is all-pervasive in time and space – present all the time everywhere.

ਸਤਿ Sat means Truth, the universal Truth, all-pervasive in time
and space; unchanging.

ਨਾਮੁ Naam has been used in two ways in Gurbani, for example: ਕਿਰਤਮ ਨਾਮ ਕਥੇ ਤੇਰੇ ਜਿਹਬਾ ॥ ਸਤਿ ਨਾਮੁ ਤੇਰਾ ਪਰਾ ਪੂਰਬਲਾ ॥ "*Kirtam naam kathey teyrey jihba; satnaam teyra paraa poorblaa*" M: 5, p 1083. The tongue/human being recounts Your names/attributes, o Almighty; but Sat-i naam-u, Your eternal writ/authority has existed from time immemorial. This shows Naam as ਨਾਮ is plural and as ਨਾਮੁ singular; plural as attributes and singular as writ/authority. According to Gurbani Vyaakran/grammar, a singular male identity has an Aunkarr as in 'ਸਤੁ' with the last letter ਤ as 'ਤੁ'. Naam used as ਨਾਮੁ in the Mool Mantar accordingly stands for Divine writ or authority. This explains the first part of Mool Mantar.

The plural ਨਾਮ refers to names given to the Almighty based on Divine attributes. The second part of Mool Mantar is an example of these like Creator, fearless, free of enmity and so on.

<u>II – The Rationlist's/Scientist's meaning of Mool Mantar.</u> *The Supreme Being whose* ***(naam-u)*** *writ/cosmic laws are* ***(sat-i = true)*** *eternal/inevitable;* ***(karta)*** *the Creator created the creation to function by Naam/cosmic laws* ***(purakh = all-pervasive)*** *which apply everywhere forever. The cosmic laws are* ***(nirbhau = without fear)*** *made to please no one, they* ***(nirvair-u = without enmity)*** *do not target anyone – i.e. everything happens systemically and not influenced by anyone. God, the Spirit behind the cosmic laws is* ***(akaal = timeless/deathless, moorat-i = embodiment)*** *Eternal* ***(ajoonee)*** *unborn and* ***(sai-bha'n)*** *self-*

*created/existent; is known (**gur = guru, prasaad-i = with grace of**) with the Guru's guidance, i.e. cosmic laws are understood with guidance of the teacher.*

The soul is a part of the Supreme Spirit, the Supreme Being.
It is sent by the Creator with the commission to perform the given duties. While away, the soul feels the pangs of separation and wants to get back. This subject of finding/reuniting with the Creator is a theme running throughout Japji and whole of Gurbani.

Note: A significant feature of Japji is that a statement made is reiterated/elaborated in later Paurris/stanzas. This will be seen as the study progresses.

॥ ਜਪੁ॥
Jap-u.

Remember and comply.

Jap-u is the name of the composition. The Vedic meaning of Jap/Jaap is to mutter something. However, the Sikh concept of Jap/Jaap is to remember/recall and obey Naam, or directions/rules to remembered and follow, like directions for travel[1]. The first

---

[1] Guru Nanak says:
ਅਜਪਾ ਜਾਪੁ ਜਪੈ ਮੁਖਿ ਨਾਮ ॥
Ajpā jāp japai mukẖ nām. M: 1, p 840

*The Brahmin should (**japai**) utter/remember Naam (**mukh-i**) with the mouth (**ajpaa jaap-u = remembrance without utterance – constant awareness**) what needs to be remembered/obeyed, (**ajpa**) without uttering (**mukh-i**) from the mouth, i.e. always keeping in mind.*

Paurri/stanza, which asks, "Kiv sachiaara hooeeai kiv koorrai tuttai paal-i; *how is one considered truthful and the wall of false-hood – impediment to union with God – is broken/removed?* And answers: Hukam rajaaee chalna Nanak likhiaa naal-i" *it is by willingly complying with Divine commands that come written with the soul.* Further, the second Paurri says 'Hukmai andar-i sabh ko baahar-i hukam-u na koey' *everyone is subject to Hukam/Divine commands/Divine writ/cosmic laws, none is outside/beyond Hukam.*

Note: The composition Jap-u starts with a prologue before Paurri 1 starts and is as follows:

ਆਦਿ ਸਚੁ ਜੁਗਾਦਿ ਸਚੁ ॥ ਹੈ ਭੀ ਸਚੁ ਨਾਨਕ ਹੋਸੀ ਭੀ ਸਚੁ ॥੧॥

Āḏ sacẖ jugāḏ sacẖ. Hai bẖī sacẖ Nānak hosī bẖī sacẖ. ||1||

The Supreme Being **(sach-u = truth/reality)** *existed, and made cosmic laws -* **(aad-i)** *before beginning of creation; has* **(sach-u = truth/reality)** *existed* **(jugaad-i)** *from the beginning of ages/time - and through the ages.*

The Eternal **(hai)** *is* **(sach-u)** *present* **(bhi)** *even now and* **(hosi bhi)** *shall also be ever present in future, -*

ਅਜਪਾ ਜਾਪੁ ਨ ਵੀਸਰੈ ਆਦਿ ਜੁਗਾਦਿ ਸਮਾਇ ॥

Ajpā jāp na vīsrai āḏ jugāḏ samā▫e. M: 1, p 1291

One then does not **(veesrai)** *forget Naam* **(ajpaa jaap-u = remembrance without utterance – constant awareness)** *which needs to be remembered/obeyed, i.e. instinctively; this way one* **(smaaey)** *remains absorbed in obedience to the Eternal Almighty who is present everywhere* **(aad-i)** *from before the beginning of time and* **(jugaad-i)** *through the ages, i.e. forever.*

and so will be Naam/cosmic laws, says Guru Nanak[1]. *1.*

In any composition, the prologue is a preface or introduction to what follows. The first prologue – for the whole of SGGS - describes the attributes of the Eternal, which the humans need to emulate to attain union with the Almighty. The rest of SGGS is an elaboration of this aspect and acts as a complete guide on all aspects of human life.

A characteristic of Jap-u is that every Paurri/stanza or group of stanzas has a context, which, generally speaking, is given in the last lines. If the context is known, understanding becomes easy.

Paurri 1

ਸੋਚੈ ਸੋਚਿ ਨ ਹੋਵਈ ਜੇ ਸੋਚੀ ਲਖ ਵਾਰ ॥

Socẖai socẖ na hova▫ī je socẖī lakẖ vār.

*The mind cannot **(soch-i)** be cleansed **(sochai)** by bathing the body even **(lakh)** a hundred thousand **(vaar)** times.*[2]

---

[1] This is restated in Paurri 27 thus: Soee soee sadaa sach-u sahib-u saachaa saachee naaee; hai bhi hosi jaaey na jaasi rachna jin-i rachaaee.

Soee soee = only that*) there is only one (**sach-u**) Eternal (**sahib-u**) Master (**sadaa**) forever, and (**naaee**) Naam/writ of (**saacha**) the Eternal (**saachi**) forever; the creation is perishable but the Creator who (**rachaai**) made it (**hai**) is present now, (**bhi hosi**) shall also be and (**jaae na jaasi**) shall not perish i.e. is Eternal.*

[2] We read in Sukhmani Sahib:

ਚੁਪੈ ਚੁਪ ਨ ਹੋਵਈ ਜੇ ਲਾਇ ਰਹਾ ਲਿਵ ਤਾਰ ॥

Cẖupai cẖup na hova▫ī je lā▫e rahā liv ṯār.

*The mind (**na hova-ee**) cannot be (**chup**) quietened even (**jey**) if I (**laaey rahaa**) remain in (**liv**) concentration (**taar**) continuously - to claim I am connected with the Eternal.*

ਭੁਖਿਆ ਭੁਖ ਨ ਉਤਰੀ ਜੇ ਬੰਨਾ ਪੁਰੀਆ ਭਾਰ ॥

Bẖukẖi▫ā bẖukẖ na uṯrī je bannā purī▫ā bẖār.

*(**Bhukhia**) those who crave, their (**bhukh = appetite**) desire for more is (**na utri = not removed**) not satiated even if they (**ba'nnaa = tie together**) gather wealth equal to (**bhaar**) the weight of all (**pureeaa**) the worlds.*[1]

ਸਹਸ ਸਿਆਣਪਾ ਲਖ ਹੋਹਿ ਤ ਇਕ ਨ ਚਲੈ ਨਾਲਿ ॥

Sahas si▫āṇpā lakẖ hohi ṯa ik na cẖalai nāl.

*One may (**hoh-i**) have (**sahas**) thousands nay (**lakh**) hundreds of thousands of (**siaanpa = wisdoms**) clever tricks, but (**ta**) then not (**ik**) one (**chalai naal-***

ਸੋਚ ਕਰੈ ਦਿਨਸੁ ਅਰੁ ਰਾਤਿ ॥ ਮਨ ਕੀ ਮੈਲੁ ਨ ਤਨ ਤੇ ਜਾਤਿ ॥

Socẖ karai ḏinas ar rāṯ. Man kī mail na ṯan ṯe jāṯ. M: 5, p 265
One may wash the body day and night, but the dirt on the mind is not removed by cleaning the body.

[1] ਬਿਨਾ ਸੰਤੋਖ ਨਹੀ ਕੋਊ ਰਾਜੈ ॥

Binā sanṯokẖ nahī ko▫ū rājai. M: 5, p 279

No one is satiated without having the quality of contentment

i) accompanies to the hereafter i.e. one who tries to be clever, can impress the world but not the Eternal.[1]

The next line asks: Then what is the solution?

ਕਿਵ ਸਚਿਆਰਾ ਹੋਈਐ ਕਿਵ ਕੂੜੈ ਤੁਟੈ ਪਾਲਿ ॥ ਹੁਕਮਿ ਰਜਾਈ ਚਲਣਾ ਨਾਨਕ ਲਿਖਿਆ ਨਾਲਿ ॥੧॥
Kiv sachiārā ho▫ī▫ai kiv kūrhai ṯutai pāl. Hukam rajā▫ī cẖalṇā Nānak likẖi▫ā nāl. ||1||

Question: ***(Kiv)*** *how* ***(paal-i)*** *the wall* ***(koorrai)*** *of falsehood, i.e. actions which separate the soul from God,* ***(tuttai)*** *is broken and one* ***(hoeeai)*** *is considered* ***(sachiaara)*** *truthful, i.e. there is no impediment to union with the Almighty.*
Answer: *It is* ***(rajaaee)*** *by willingly* ***(chalna = moving)*** *conducting the self* ***(hukam-i)*** *according to Divine commands which came* ***(likhiaa)*** *written* ***(naal-i)*** *with the soul, i.e. present in the mind as conscience; there are rules for every type of role*[2]*. 1.*

---

[1] ਹਉ ਪੰਡਿਤੁ ਹਉ ਚਤੁਰੁ ਸਿਆਣਾ ॥ ਕਰਣੈਹਾਰੁ ਨ ਬੁਝੈ ਬਿਗਾਨਾ ॥੩॥

Ha▫o pandiṯ ha▫o cẖaṯur si▫āṇā. Karṇaihār na bujẖai bigānā. 3. M: 5, p 178.

One says "I am a scholar, clever and wise, never care to find the Creator within and remains ignorant."

[2] The fourth Guru elucidates it thus:
ਸਭੁ ਜੀਉ ਪਿੰਡੁ ਦੀਆ ਤੁਧੁ ਆਪੇ ਤੁਧੁ ਆਪੇ ਕਾਰੈ ਲਾਇਆ ॥ ਜੇਹਾ ਤੂੰ ਹੁਕਮੁ ਕਰਹਿ ਤੇਹੇ ਕੋ ਕਰਮ ਕਮਾਵੈ ਜੇਹਾ ਤੁਧੁ ਧੁਰਿ ਲਿਖਿ ਪਾਇਆ ॥੨॥
Sabẖ jī▫o pind ḏī▫ā ṯuḏẖ āpe ṯuḏẖ āpe kārai lā▫i▫ā. Jehā ṯūʼn hukam karahi ṯehe ko karam kamāvai jehā ṯuḏẖ ḏẖur likẖ pā▫i▫ā. ||2||

Ego is the wall of falsehood mentioned above. This means ignoring Hukam and acting by self-will, comes in way of union with the Creator.

Paurri 2

ਹੁਕਮੀ ਹੋਵਨਿ ਆਕਾਰ ਹੁਕਮੁ ਨ ਕਹਿਆ ਜਾਈ ॥

Hukmī hovan ākār hukam na kahiᵒā jāᵒī.

*All **(aakaar)** physical forms **(hovan)** come into being **(hukami)** by Divine command; but **(na jaaee)** it is not possible **(kahia)** to say how wide this **(hukam)** command applies, i.e. expanse of creation is not known.*

ਹੁਕਮੀ ਹੋਵਨਿ ਜੀਅ ਹੁਕਮਿ ਮਿਲੈ ਵਡਿਆਈ ॥

Hukmī hovan jīᵒa hukam milai vadiᵒāᵒī.

*All **(jee-a)** creatures **(hovan)** come into being **(hukmi)** by Divine command - what role they are to perform in life - since they are part of creation, they conform to natural laws; those who live **(hukam-i)** by Divine commands/the natural laws **(milai)** receive **(vadiaai = praise)** glory with the Creator/are at peace.*

(Tudh-u) *You* ***(aapey)*** *Yourself* ***(deeaa)*** *gave* ***(jeeo)*** *the soul/mind and* ***(pindd-u)*** *body and Yourself* ***(laaiaa = engaged)*** *allotted* ***(kaarai)*** *the task/role in life to everyone.* ***(Jeyha = whatever type)*** *whatever* ***(hukam-u)*** *command* ***(too-n)*** *You* ***(karah-i)*** *give,* ***(ko)*** *someone* ***(kamavai)*** *carries out* ***(karam = deed)*** *the task* ***(teyho = same type)*** *accordingly,* ***(jeyha)*** *as* ***(tudh-u)*** *You* ***(likh-i paaiaa)*** *have written and put* ***(dhur-i)*** *from the source, i.e. at birth. 2.*

ਹੁਕਮੀ ਉਤਮੁ ਨੀਚੁ ਹੁਕਮਿ ਲਿਖਿ ਦੁਖ ਸੁਖ ਪਾਈਅਹਿ ॥

Hukmī uṯam nīcẖ hukam likẖ ḏukẖ sukẖ pā▫ī▫ah.

*It is (**hukmee**) by Hukam that one acts (**utam-u**) sublime by Naam, or (**neech-u = low**) disobeys Naam; this is (**likh-i**) inscribe in one's nature and (**hukam-i**) by Hukam/Divine law – of one reaps what one sows – and (**paaeeah-i**) are accordingly experiences (**dukh**) distress/restless-ness or (**sukh**) comfort/peace.*

ਇਕਨਾ ਹੁਕਮੀ ਬਖਸੀਸ ਇਕਿ ਹੁਕਮੀ ਸਦਾ ਭਵਾਈਅਹਿ ॥

Iknā hukmī bakẖsīs ik hukmī saḏā bẖavā▫ī▫ah.

*(**Ikna = one type**) those who obey are bestowed (**bakhsees**) grace - are united with the Creator - while (**ikna**) others (**bhavaaeeah-i = caused to go in circles**) are kept in cycles of births and deaths (**sadaa**) ever – they are those who do not comply with Naam*[1]. The Paurri concludes thus:

ਹੁਕਮੈ ਅੰਦਰਿ ਸਭੁ ਕੋ ਬਾਹਰਿ ਹੁਕਮ ਨ ਕੋਇ ॥ ਨਾਨਕ ਹੁਕਮੈ ਜੇ ਬੁਝੈ ਤ ਹਉਮੈ ਕਹੈ ਨ ਕੋਇ ॥੨॥

---

[1] Japji Paurri 20 says: ॥ ਆਪੇ ਬੀਜਿ ਆਪੇ ਹੀ ਖਾਹੁ ॥ ਨਾਨਕ ਹੁਕਮੀ ਆਵਹੁ ਜਾਹੁ ॥੨੦॥

Āpe bīj āpe hī kẖāhu. Nānak hukmī āvhu jāhu. ||20||

*Consequences are imposed based on the principle that what (**aapey = self**) one (**beejai**) sows, (**hi**) only s/he (**aapey**) him/her-self (**khaah-u = eats**) gets/faces the consequences. One who transgresses (**aavhu = comes**) is born and (**jaah-u = goes**) dies again and again, (**hukmi = by orders**) by Divine commands, says Guru Nanak. 20.*

Hukmai andar sabh ko bāhar hukam na ko▫e. Nānak hukmai je bujhai ta ha▫umai kahai na ko▫e. ||2||

*(**Sabh ko**) everyone is (**andar-i = within**) subject (**hukmai**) to Hukam; (**na koey = not any**) none is (**baahar-i = outside**) beyond Hukam.*
*Says Nanak: (**Jey**) if one (**bujhai**) understands/obeys (**hukmai**) Hukam/Divine commands, (**ta**) then s/he does (**kahai**) says (**na koey**) nothing (**haumai**) in ego i.e. does not claim to be the doer, or do things by his/her own will. 2.*

Paurri 3

It is natural to express gratitude to anyone who helps one. The Almighty has provided everything for the creatures. A thoughtful humble person realises this and praises the Almighty as the beneficent Creator and Sustainor. This leads to development of faith in, and obedience of, the Master. This is the subject of Paurri 3. The expression used for this is Gaavai meaning sings or praises/acknowledges and obeys. It happens according to one's understanding or experience.

ਗਾਵੈ ਕੋ ਤਾਣੁ ਹੋਵੈ ਕਿਸੈ ਤਾਣੁ ॥ ਗਾਵੈ ਕੋ ਦਾਤਿ ਜਾਣੈ ਨੀਸਾਣੁ ॥
Gāvai ko tāṇ hovai kisai tāṇ.Gāvai ko dāt jāṇai nīsāṇ.

*(**Ko**) someone (**gaavai = sings**) praises God asking for some (**taan-u**) strength/capability; (**kisai**) someone praises God for (**hovai = happens**) having got (**taan-u = strength**) the ability, i.e. has achieved something, then s/he praises the Almighty.*
*(**Ko**) someone (**gaavai = sings**) praises the Almighty (**jaanai**) taking/seeing (**daat-i**) a benediction received, as (**neesaan-u**) sign of God's benevolence, say good health, family or wealth.*

ਗਾਵੈ ਕੋ ਗੁਣ ਵਡਿਆਈਆ ਚਾਰ ॥ ਗਾਵੈ ਕੋ ਵਿਦਿਆ ਵਿਖਮੁ ਵੀਚਾਰੁ ॥
Gāvai ko guṇ vaḏi▫ā▫ī▫ā cẖār. Gāvai ko viḏi▫ā vikẖam vīcẖār.

*Someone (**gaavai**) praises marvelling at (**chaar**) the beautiful/wondrous (**gun**) attributes/powers and (**vaddiaaeeaa = greatness**) majesty of God.*
*Someone praises God for having (**vikham-u = difficult**) hard-to-obtain (**vidiaa**) knowledge and (**veechaar-u**) reflects on it.*

ਗਾਵੈ ਕੋ ਸਾਜਿ ਕਰੇ ਤਨੁ ਖੇਹ ॥ ਗਾਵੈ ਕੋ ਜੀਅ ਲੈ ਫਿਰਿ ਦੇਹ ॥
Gāvai ko sāj kare ṯan kẖeh. Gāvai ko jī▫a lai fir ḏeh.

*Someone praises Divine powers to (**saaj-i**) create (**tan-u**) the body and then (**karey = makes, kheyh = dust**) destroy.*
*Someone praises seeing God's powers to (**lai**) take (**jeea**) life and (**phir-i**) then (**deyh = give**) restore it.*
Note: It means that God causes some to fall prey to temptations and gives strength to some to overcome them.

ਗਾਵੈ ਕੋ ਜਾਪੈ ਦਿਸੈ ਦੂਰਿ ॥ ਗਾਵੈ ਕੋ ਵੇਖੈ ਹਾਦਰਾ ਹਦੂਰਿ ॥
Gāvai ko jāpai ḏisai ḏūr. Gāvai ko vekẖai hāḏrā haḏūr.

*Someone (**jaapai = seems, disai = is seen**) perceives God (**door-i**) far away, and (**gaavai**) praises – as being high, beyond reach, and wishes to find.*
*Someone (**veykhai**) sees God present (**haadraa/haazra hadoor/hazoor**) right before him/her, and (**gaavai**) praises God – when s/he experiences Divine presence within.*

ਕਥਨਾ ਕਥੀ ਨ ਆਵੈ ਤੋਟਿ ॥ ਕਥਿ ਕਥਿ ਕਥੀ ਕੋਟੀ ਕੋਟਿ ਕੋਟਿ ॥
Kathnā kathī na āvai tot. Kath kath kathī kotī kot kot.

*(**Kathee**) describing (**kathnee = description**) virtues and powers of God does not (**tott-i**) end. (**Kottee kott-i kott-i = many crores**) countless people (**kath-i kath-i kathee**) keep describing[1].*

ਦੇਦਾ ਦੇ ਲੈਦੇ ਥਕਿ ਪਾਹਿ ॥ ਜੁਗਾ ਜੁਗੰਤਰਿ ਖਾਹੀ ਖਾਹਿ ॥
Ḏeḏā ḏe laiḏe thak pāhi. Jugā juganṯar kẖāhī kẖāhi.

*(**Deyda = giver**) the Almighty keeps (**dey**) giving and the creatures (**thak-i paah-i**) get tired of (**laidey**) receiving, i.e. they receive until they die. They (**khaahee khaahh-i**) eat/receive the wherewithal (**juga jagantar-i = in age after age**) in birth after birth.*

ਹੁਕਮੀ ਹੁਕਮੁ ਚਲਾਏ ਰਾਹੁ ॥ ਨਾਨਕ ਵਿਗਸੈ ਵੇਪਰਵਾਹੁ ॥੩॥
Hukmī hukam cẖalā▫e rāhu. Nānak vigsai veparvāhu. ||3||

---

[1] Guru Nanak says elsewhere: ਕਿਆ ਹਉ ਕਥੀ ਕਥੇ ਕਥਿ ਦੇਖਾ ਮੈ ਅਕਥੁ ਨ ਕਥਨਾ ਜਾਈ ॥ ਜੋ ਤੁਧੁ ਭਾਵੈ ਸੋਈ ਆਖਾ ਤਿਲੁ ਤੇਰੀ ਵਡਿਆਈ ॥੩॥

Ki▫ā ha▫o kathī kathe kath ḏekẖā mai akath na kathnā jā▫ī. Jo ṯuḏẖ bẖāvai so▫ī ākẖā ṯil ṯerī vadi▫ā▫ī. ||3||

*(**Kiaa**) what can (**hau**) I (**kathi**) say; I have tried (**kathey kath-i**) to describe, but (**deykha = seen**) found that You are (**akath-u**) beyond description and (**na jaaee**) cannot (**kathna**) be described.*
*(**Jo**) whatever (**bhaavai**) pleases (**tudh-u**) You, i.e. whatever awareness You give, I (**aakhaa**) say (**soi**) that (**til-u = equal to sesame seed**) bit, in (**teyri**) Your (**vaddiaaee**) praise. 3. M: 1, p 795.*

*(**Hukam-u = order**) commands of (**hukmi = one with authority to order**) the Master (**chalaaey = causes to move**) has laid down commands/roles for all types of creatures.*

*Says Guru Nanak: The Master (**vigsai**) is happy to watch the creation but is (**veyparvaahu**) carefree, i.e. has no attachments or expectation. 3.*

Paurri 4.

Most people pray to God to ask for something. This was mentioned in Paurri 3, and is repeated in Paurri 4. However wittingly or unwittingly, God is perceived to be like a person who needs to be pleased to give favours. Making offerings and singing paeans are practiced in this regard. Keeping this in view, Guru Nanak asks a question, and answers:

ਸਾਚਾ ਸਾਹਿਬੁ ਸਾਚੁ ਨਾਇ ਭਾਖਿਆ ਭਾਉ ਅਪਾਰੁ ॥ ਆਖਹਿ ਮੰਗਹਿ ਦੇਹਿ ਦੇਹਿ ਦਾਤਿ ਕਰੇ ਦਾਤਾਰੁ ॥

Sācẖā sāhib sācẖ nā▫e bẖākẖi▫ā bẖā▫o apār. Ākẖahi mangahi ḏehi ḏehi ḏāṯ kare ḏāṯār.

*(**Saacha**) the Eternal (**sahib-u**) Master whose (**naaey**) Naam/commands are (**saach-u**) eternal, i.e. whose writ ever applies everywhere, is (**bhaakhia = spoken**) praised with (**apaar-u**) infinite (**bhaau**) love by the seekers.*

*The mortals praise the Master, and (**mangeyh**) beg (**aakhah-i = say**) saying (**deyh-i deyh-i**) give us, give us; (**daataar-u = giver**) the beneficent Master (**karey**) grants (**daat-i**) benedictions.*

ਫੇਰਿ ਕਿ ਅਗੈ ਰਖੀਐ ਜਿਤੁ ਦਿਸੈ ਦਰਬਾਰੁ ॥ ਮੁਹੌ ਕਿ ਬੋਲਣੁ ਬੋਲੀਐ ਜਿਤੁ ਸੁਣਿ ਧਰੇ ਪਿਆਰੁ ॥

Fer kė agai rakẖī▫ai jiṯ ḏisai ḏarbār. Muhou kė bolaṇ bolī▫ai jiṯ suṇ ḏẖare pi▫ār.

Question: The Almighty is so benevolent; the seeker wishes to have vision the Master: ***(Pheyr)*** *then* ***(k-i)*** *what offering should* ***(rakheeai)*** *be placed* ***(agai)*** *before the Beneficent Master* ***(jit-u)*** *by which* ***(darbaar = court)*** *Divine presence* ***(disai)*** *is seen, i.e. vision of God is enabled?*
(K-i) *what* ***(bolan-u)*** *word should one* ***(boleeai)*** *say* ***(muhou)*** *from the mouth, i.e. what words of glorification/supplication should be uttered, what mantra should be chanted,* ***(sun-i)*** *hearing which the Almighty* ***(dharey)*** *bears* ***(piaar-u)*** *love, i.e. is pleased.*

Note: Guru Nanak asks if making offerings, entreaties and chanting mantras enables to find the Almighty. And, says no; the following does.

ਅੰਮ੍ਰਿਤ ਵੇਲਾ ਸਚੁ ਨਾਉ ਵਡਿਆਈ ਵੀਚਾਰੁ ॥
Amriṯ velā sacẖ nā▫o vadi▫ā▫ī vīcẖār.

Answer: The Almighty expects nothing material and is not pleased by paeans, but by one's conduct, therefore: ***(Veechaar-u)*** *reflect on* ***(vaddiaaee)*** *greatness/importance of conformance to* ***(sach-u)*** *eternal/inevitable* ***(naau)*** *Naam/commands of the Master in* ***(amrit)*** *the ambrosial* ***(veyla = time)*** *hours of the morning – and conduct yourself by them day and night.*

Note: It is significant that the guru is asking to reflect on Naam in the morning. Reflection needs absence of distractions. This is in the morning before one gets involved in mundane activities of the day.

Contemplation on Naam/commands is needed to understand them as guide for life.

ਕਰਮੀ ਆਵੈ ਕਪੜਾ ਨਦਰੀ ਮੋਖੁ ਦੁਆਰੁ ॥ ਨਾਨਕ ਏਵੈ ਜਾਣੀਐ ਸਭੁ ਆਪੇ ਸਚਿਆਰੁ ॥੪॥

Karmī āvai kapṛā nadrī mokẖ ḏuār. Nānak evai jāṇīai sabẖ āpe sacẖiār.

*(**Kaprra = garment – cover for the soul**) a life form (**aavai = comes**) is obtained (**karmi**) based on deeds; (**mokh-u**) emancipation, i.e. liberation from being born, and entry to (**duaar-u = gate**) the Divine abode/union with the Almighty, is obtained (**nadree**) by Divine grace – which is deserved by obedience.*
*(**Eyvai**) this is how – by Divine grace - one (**jaaneeai = knows**) recognizes/understands that (**sachiaar-u**) the Eternal Master is (**aapey**) IT-self present (**sabh-u**) everywhere, - and one obeys Divine writ/cosmic laws everywhere – and thus temptations are kept at bay. 4.*

Paurri 5

Paurri 5 says the Almighty cannot be ਥਾਪਿਆ (**thaapia**) installed. This refers to images or idols of deities installed in temples and other places, and worshipped. It also says the Almighty cannot be ਕੀਤਾ (**keeta**) created/born, i.e. is not a person. This reiterates the Ajooni/unborn and Saibh'n/self-created attributes of the Creator in the Mool Mantar.

ਥਾਪਿਆ ਨ ਜਾਇ ਕੀਤਾ ਨ ਹੋਇ ॥ ਆਪੇ ਆਪਿ ਨਿਰੰਜਨੁ ਸੋਇ ॥

Thāpiā na jāe kīṯā na hoe. Āpe āp niranjan soe.

*The Almighty **(na jaaey)** cannot be **(thaapia)** installed – like an idol; God **(na hoey)** cannot be **(keeta)** created, i.e. is unborn.*
*(**Soey = that one**) the One Master is (**aapey aap-i**) self-created/self-existent and (**niranjan-u = un-stained**) is the pristine Supreme Spirit, i.e. does not have physical form and is untouched by the goings on in the world.*

ਜਿਨਿ ਸੇਵਿਆ ਤਿਨਿ ਪਾਇਆ ਮਾਨੁ ॥ ਨਾਨਕ ਗਾਵੀਐ ਗੁਣੀ ਨਿਧਾਨੁ ॥
Jin sevi▫ā ṯin pā▫i▫ā mān. Nānak gāvī▫ai guṇī niḏẖān.

*(**Jin-i**) one who (**seyviaa = serves**) obeys Naam/commands of the Master, (**paaiaa**) receives (**maan-u**) recognition/honour – from people in the world, being at peace with the self, and by way of approval for union by God.*
*We should therefore (**gaaveeai = sing**) praise – acknowledge and obey the Almighty, (**nidhaan-u = treasure**) the fountainhead (**guni**) of virtues, says Guru Nanak.*

ਗਾਵੀਐ ਸੁਣੀਐ ਮਨਿ ਰਖੀਐ ਭਾਉ ॥
Gāvī▫ai suṇī▫ai man rakẖī▫ai bẖā▫o.

*We should (**gaaveeai = sing**) praise/acknowledge the Master;*
*(**suneeai**) listen to Naam– attend holy congregation and reflect within.*
*(**Man-i**) accept/obey, and (**rakheeai**) keep Naam (**bhaau**) lovingly (**man-i**) in mind – in thought, word and deed.*

ਦੁਖੁ ਪਰਹਰਿ ਸੁਖੁ ਘਰਿ ਲੈ ਜਾਇ ॥
Ḏukẖ parhar sukẖ gẖar lai jā▫e.

*This (**parhar-i**) banishes (**dukh-u**) the pain - of continued separation from the Creator, and (**lai jaaey**) takes to (**sukh-u**) comfort (**ghar-i**) of the home, i.e. ends restless-ness and brings peace with the mind fixed on the Creator. This happens by driving out other ideas and discovering Naam within.*

Note: The next line Guru Nanak takes note that the Sanaatan Dharma concept of the guru giving (**naad = sound**) guru mantra into the ear to chant and of rituals contained (**veyd = Vedas**) in texts to find God, and says:

ਗੁਰਮੁਖਿ ਨਾਦੰ ਗੁਰਮੁਖਿ ਵੇਦੰ ਗੁਰਮੁਖਿ ਰਹਿਆ ਸਮਾਈ ॥
Gurmukẖ nāḏaʼn gurmukẖ veḏaʼn gurmukẖ rahi▫ā samā▫ī.

*Real spiritual experience comes by following (**gurmukh-i = from the guru's mouth**) the guru's teachings – of living by Naam -, rather than through (**naada'n**) chanting of mantras or performing rituals given (**veyda'n**) the Vedas. (**gurmukh-i**) the Guru's guidance brings awareness of the Almighty (**rahiaa samaaee**) being present is everywhere[1].*

---

[1] Guru Nanak reaffirms this thus:
ਸਭਿ ਨਾਦ ਬੇਦ ਗੁਰਬਾਣੀ ॥ ਮਨੁ ਰਾਤਾ ਸਾਰਿਗਪਾਣੀ ॥ ਤਹ ਤੀਰਥ ਵਰਤ ਤਪ ਸਾਰੇ ॥ ਗੁਰ ਮਿਲਿਆ ਹਰਿ ਨਿਸਤਾਰੇ ॥੩॥
Sabẖ nāḏ beḏ gurbāṇī. Man rāṯā sārigpāṇī. Ŧah ṯirath varaṯ ṯap sāre. Gur mili▫ā har nisṯāre. ||3||

*The Yogi says (**naad**) music connects him to God and the Pandit believes (**beyd = Veda**) scriptural reading does; for me, (**gurbani**) the guru's word is (**sabh-i**) all Naad and B-ed; with it, (**man**) the mind is (**raata**) imbued with love of (**saarigpaani = provider of water for the rain bird**) the Almighty.*

ਗੁਰੁ ਈਸਰੁ ਗੁਰੁ ਗੋਰਖੁ ਬਰਮਾ ਗੁਰੁ ਪਾਰਬਤੀ ਮਾਈ ॥
Gur īsar gur gorakẖ barmā gur pārbaṯī mā▫ī.

But the seeker follows **(gur-u)** *the guru's teachings instead of worshipping-*

(Barma = Brahma) *as creator - the guru creates awareness of virtues of the Almighty.*
(Eesar = Shankar/Mahadev/Shiva) *as destroyer - the guru destroys ignorance.*
(Gorakh = Vishnu) *as preserver - the guru that we should keep virtues of the Almighty in mind to be safe from evil.*
(Paarbati maaee = mother goddess) *goddess Parvathi/Durga/Lakshmi/Sarswati. (*Note: Stories in Hindu texts say that whenever gods are troubled by the demons, they seek help of the goddess. Lakshmi is the goddess of wealth and Sarswati that of knowledge*). The guru imparts awareness of Naam and keeps evil away.*

Note: Gorakh Nath is also the name of the head of the Nath Yogis. However Gorakh originally stands for Vishnu (go + rakh = preserver of the earth) the sustainer in Hindu trinity; the other two namely Brahma and Shiva are mentioned here as Eesar and

---

(Saarey) *all* ***(teerath)*** *pilgrimages,* ***(varat)*** *fasts and* ***(tap)*** *austerities are covered in* ***(tah = there)*** *that, i.e. there is no need for them. Those who* ***(miliaa)*** *find the guru and follow him,* ***(har-i)*** *the Almighty* ***(nistaarey = takes across the night – overnight stop for the soul)*** *emancipates them from rebirth in the world. 3. M: 1, 879.*

Teerath/pilgrimage mentioned above reiterates what Japji Paurri 6 below says.

Barma. Guru Nanak tells the Yogis elsewhere; you say Gorakh is your guru, but Gorakh represents the Sustainor Almighty.[1]

The Paurri further says:

ਜੇ ਹਉ ਜਾਣਾ ਆਖਾ ਨਾਹੀ ਕਹਣਾ ਕਥਨੁ ਨ ਜਾਈ ॥
Je ha▫o jāṇā ākẖā nāhī kahṇā kathan na jā▫ī.

*The guru's teachings are enlightening, but **(jey)** if I **(jaana = know)** experience the Almighty with the guru's guidance, I will not be able to **(aakhaa)** express, because the Master **(na jaa-ee)** cannot **(kahna kathan)** be described in words – presence of the Almighty can only be experienced not described[2].*

ਗੁਰਾ ਇਕ ਦੇਹਿ ਬੁਝਾਈ ॥ ਸਭਨਾ ਜੀਆ ਕਾ ਇਕੁ ਦਾਤਾ ਸੋ ਮੈ ਵਿਸਰਿ ਨ ਜਾਈ ॥੫॥

---

1 ਬਾਬਾ ਗੋਰਖੁ ਜਾਗੈ ॥ ਗੋਰਖੁ ਸੋ ਜਿਨਿ ਗੋਇ ਉਠਾਲੀ ਕਰਤੇ ਬਾਰ ਨ ਲਾਗੈ ॥੧॥ ਰਹਾਉ ॥
Bābā gorakẖ jāgai. Gorakẖ so jin go▫e uṯẖālī karṯe bār na lāgai. ||1|| rahā▫o.
O (baaba) dear, (gorakh-u = protector of earth) the Almighty (jaagai) is awake – ever looks after the creation.

The Nath Yogis call their mentor Gorakh Nath, but; for the seeker *Gorakh is the One Almighty who supports the world; IT takes no (baar) time in doing what IT desires.* 1. M: 1, 877.

2 Paurri 26 says:
ਏਤੇ ਕੀਤੇ ਹੋਰਿ ਕਰੇਹਿ ॥ ਤਾ ਆਖਿ ਨ ਸਕਹਿ ਕੇਈ ਕੇਇ ॥
Ėṯe kīṯe hor karehi. Ŧā ākẖ na sakahi ke▫ī ke▫e.

*The Creator **(keetey)** created **(eytey)** these many and if **(karah-i)** creates **(hor-i)** more; even **(ta)** then **(na keyee key-i = not any)** no one **(sakah-i)** can **(aakh-i = say)** describe virtues and powers of the Almighty.*

Gurā ik ḏehi bujẖā▫ī. Sabẖnā jī▫ā kā ik ḏāṯā so mai visar na jā▫ī. ||5||

*(**Guraa**) the guru (**deyh-i**) has given me this (**ik**) one thing (**bujhaaee**) to understand.*
*That there is only (**ik-u**) One (**daata = giver**) beneficent Master of all (**jeeaa = creatures**) living beings; (**mai**) I should not (**visar jaaee**) forget IT.*

Note: Some works translate by as "Guraa ik deyh-i bujhaaee" as "o' guru give me this one understanding". A little reflection would show that one cannot be telling the guru what understanding to give – asking for enlightenment is different. Paurri 6, says the Naam-jewel is present in mind but the creature remains unaware. One who listens to the guru becomes aware it..

Paurri 6

Many faiths prescribe going on pilgrimages. Jerusalem is called the holy land by all Semitic faiths and great importance is given to going on pilgrimage there. Muslims have Hajj, i.e. pilgrimage to Mecca/Makkah in Saudi Arabia at least once in lifetime, prescribed as one of the five basic tenets of their faith. Similarly taking baths in rivers like Ganga, Jamna/Yamuna, specifically at Haridwar, Kaashi/Banaras or the Sangam at Allahabad, is widely practiced in Hindu faith. Some days like Makkar Sakraanti in the middle of January has special importance. This is believed to purify the mind as a means to find God. However, the mind cannot be cleansed by bathing the body or other rituals like visits. They only generate pride[1].

---

[1] ਮ: ੧ ॥ ਨਾਵਣ ਚਲੇ ਤੀਰਥੀ ਮਨਿ ਖੋਟੈ ਤਨਿ ਚੋਰ ॥ ਇਕੁ ਭਾਉ ਲਥੀ ਨਾਤਿਆ ਦੁਇ ਭਾ ਚੜੀਅਸੁ ਹੋਰ ॥

Mėhlā 1. Nāvaṇ c̲hale t̲īrthī man kh̲otai t̲an c̲hor. Ik bh̲ā▫o lathī nāt̲i▫ā d̲u▫e bh̲ā c̲haṛī▫as hor.

*Prologue by the first Guru: Some people (**khottey** = **counterfeit**) have evil (**man-i**) in mind and (**chor** = **thieves**) are evil (**tan-i** = **body**) by deeds but (**chaley**) go to (**naavan**) bathe (**teerthi**) at pilgrimages - to show piety i.e. they pretend to be what they are not.*
*While (**ik-u**) one (**bhaau** = **idea**) thing – dirt of the body (**lathi**) is removed, (**duey-i**) twice (**hor**) more of (**bhaa** = **ideas**) the dirt of false pride of piety (**charreeas-u** = **put on**) is added, i.e. the result is negative.*M: 1, p 789

Guru Nanak also says:

ਤੀਰਥਿ ਨਾਵਣ ਜਾਉ ਤੀਰਥੁ ਨਾਮੁ ਹੈ ॥ ਤੀਰਥੁ ਸਬਦ ਬੀਚਾਰੁ ਅੰਤਰਿ ਗਿਆਨੁ ਹੈ ॥
Ŧirath nāvaṇ jā▫o t̲irath nām hai. Ŧirath sabad̲ bīc̲hār ant̲ar gi▫ān hai.

*I (**jaau**) go to (**naavan-u**) bathe (**teerth-i**) at places of pilgrimage; that (**teerath-i**) pilgrimage is washing vices off the mind by emulating (**naam-u**) Divine virtues.*
*Pilgrimage is (**beechaar-u**) to contemplate (**sabad** = **Divine Word**) Divine commands and (**hai**) is to get their (**giaan-u**) awareness (**antar-i**) within. M: 1, p 687.*

This is similar to Paurri 4 saying;
Amrit̲ velā sac̲h nā▫o vadi▫ā▫ī vīc̲hār.

Answer: *(**Veechaar-u**) reflect on/comply with (**sach-u**) eternal/inevitable (**naau**) Naam/commands and (**vaddiaaee**) virtues of the Master in (**amrit**) the ambrosial (**veyla** = **time**) hours of the morning – and conduct yourself by them day and night.*

And Paurri 21, which says:

ਸੁਣਿਆ ਮੰਨਿਆ ਮਨਿ ਕੀਤਾ ਭਾਉ ॥ ਅੰਤਰਗਤਿ ਤੀਰਥਿ ਮਲਿ ਨਾਉ ॥
Suṇi▫ā mani▫ā man kīt̲ā bh̲ā▫o. Ant̲argat̲ t̲irath mal nā▫o.

*One who (**ma'nniaa**) listens, (**ma'nniaa**) obeys and (**keetaa bhaau** = **does with love**) lovingly keeps Naam (**man-i**) in*

The mind is purified by humbly submitting to Naam, and giving up other ideas with the guru's guidance. This is the subject of Paurri 6.

ਤੀਰਥਿ ਨਾਵਾ ਜੇ ਤਿਸੁ ਭਾਵਾ ਵਿਣੁ ਭਾਣੇ ਕਿ ਨਾਇ ਕਰੀ ॥

Ŧirath nāvā je ṯis bẖāvā viṇ bẖāṇe kė nā▫e karī.

*I should (**naava/nhaava**) bathe (**teerath-i**) at pilgrimages to holy places (**jey**) if I (**bhaava**) receive approval of (**tis-u = that**) the Almighty; (**k-i**) what use is (**naaey karee**) bathing, i.e. performing rituals (**vin-u = without**) if one is not, (**bhaaney**) being liked by the Master, i.e. if the mind is clean enough for the Almighty to abide.*

ਜੇਤੀ ਸਿਰਠਿ ਉਪਾਈ ਵੇਖਾ ਵਿਣੁ ਕਰਮਾ ਕਿ ਮਿਲੈ ਲਈ ॥

Jeṯī siraṯẖ upā▫ī vekẖā viṇ karmā kė milai la▫ī.

*In (**jeyti = as much**) the whole (**sirth-i/sristi = universe**) humankind (**upaaee**) created by the Creator, let me (**veykha**) see, (**k-i**) what can anyone (**milai**) get (**vin-u**) without (**karma = deeds**) working for it? If (**milai**) it is obtained, then let anyone (**laee**) take.*

ਮਤਿ ਵਿਚਿ ਰਤਨ ਜਵਾਹਰ ਮਾਣਿਕ ਜੇ ਇਕ ਗੁਰ ਕੀ ਸਿਖ ਸੁਣੀ ॥

Maṯ vicẖ raṯan javāhar māṇik je ik gur kī sikẖ suṇī.

---

*mind – to conform to Naam in all activities; s/he (**naau = bathes**) washes off (**mal-i**) the dirt of evil from within (**teerath-i**) at the pilgrimage of (**antargat-i = antar = inside + gat-i = freedom**) inner purification – this is how God is experienced within.*

(Ratan, javaahar, maanik = precious stones) *jewels and gems of awareness of Naam/Divine virtues and commands - are present **(vich-i)** in the **(mat-i = intellect)** human mind – and one becomes aware of them - **(jey)** if one **(sunee)** listens to **(sikh)** the teachings **(ki)** of **(ik-u = one)** the true guru[1] – who frees from delusion, to recognize Naam within.*

ਗੁਰਾ ਇਕ ਦੇਹਿ ਬੁਝਾਈ ॥ ਸਭਨਾ ਜੀਆ ਕਾ ਇਕੁ ਦਾਤਾ ਸੋ ਮੈ ਵਿਸਰਿ ਨ ਜਾਈ ॥੬॥

Gurā ik ḏehi bujẖā▫ī. Sabẖnā jī▫ā kā ik ḏāṯā so mai visar na jā▫ī. ||6||

***(Guraa)** the guru **(deyh-i)** has given me this **(ik)** one thing **(bujhaaee)** to understand.*
*That there is only **(ik-u)** One beneficent Master **(daata = giver)** Creator and Sustainor of all **(jeeaa = creatures)** living beings;*

---

[1] The fourth Guru says:
ਰਤਨੁ ਜਵੇਹਰੁ ਲਾਲੁ ਹਰਿ ਨਾਮਾ ਗੁਰਿ ਕਾਢਿ ਤਲੀ ਦਿਖਲਾਇਆ ॥ ਭਾਗਹੀਣ ਮਨਮੁਖਿ ਨਹੀ ਲੀਆ ਤ੍ਰਿਣ ਓਲੈ ਲਾਖੁ ਛਪਾਇਆ ॥੩॥
Raṯan javehar lāl har nāmā gur kādẖ ṯalī ḏikẖlā▫i▫ā. Bẖāghīṇ manmukẖ nahī lī▫ā ṯariṇ olai lākẖ cẖẖapā▫i▫ā. ||3||

***(Gur-i)** the guru **(kaaddh-i)** brings out from within, i.e. imparts awareness of, **(ratan-u = jewel, javeyhar-u = emerald, and laal-u = ruby)** the priceless **(har-i naama)** Divine virtues and commands, and **(dikhlaaiaa)** shows by placing **(tali)** on palm of the hand, i.e. imparts awareness of Naam.*
***(Manmukh-i = self-willed)** those who do not follow the guru are **(bhaag-heen)** unfortunate; they do not **(leeaa = take)** get awareness as **(laakkh-u = one hundred thousand)** priceless Naam **(chhapaaiaa)** remains hidden behind **(trin = straw)** the worthless thoughts of attachments to the world-play. 3. M: 4, p 880.*

*May (**mai**) I never (**visar jaaee**) forget (**so**) that, i.e. Naam – directions on how to lead life. 6.*

<u>Paurri 7</u>

This Paurri cautions not to be obsessed with glory of worldly status. It does not help when the soul is evaluated for deeds.

ਜੇ ਜੁਗ ਚਾਰੇ ਆਰਜਾ ਹੋਰ ਦਸੂਣੀ ਹੋਇ ॥

Je jug c̱ẖāre ārjā hor ḏasūṇī ho▫e.

*(**Jey**) if (**aarja**) life of a person (**hoey**) be as long as (**chaarey**) all four (**jug/Yug**) ages, i.e. millions of years, or be (**dasoonee**) ten-times (**hor**) more.*

ਨਵਾ ਖੰਡਾ ਵਿਚਿ ਜਾਣੀਐ ਨਾਲਿ ਚਲੈ ਸਭੁ ਕੋਇ ॥

Navā kẖanda vicẖ jāṇī▫ai nāl c̱ẖalai sabẖ ko▫e.

*And, s/he is (**jaaneeai = known**) famous (**vich-i**) in (**navaa**) all nine (**khanddaa**) planets, i.e. the whole, the universe, and (**sabh-u koey**) every one (**chalai**) walks (**naal-i**) with him/her, i.e. wants to be seen with him/her.*

ਚੰਗਾ ਨਾਉ ਰਖਾਇ ਕੈ ਜਸੁ ਕੀਰਤਿ ਜਗਿ ਲੇਇ ॥

C̱ẖanga nā▫o rakẖā▫e kai jas kīraṯ jag le▫e.

*S/he acts such as (**rakhaaey kai**) to get (**changa**) good (**naau = name**) reputation, and (**ley-i**) receives (**jas-u**) praise and (**keerat-i**) fame (**jag-i**) in the world.*

ਜੇ ਤਿਸੁ ਨਦਰਿ ਨ ਆਵਈ ਤ ਵਾਤ ਨ ਪੁਛੈ ਕੇ ॥

Je ṯis naḏar na āvī ṯa vāṯ na pucẖẖai ke.

*But, (**jey**) if (**nadar-i**) grace of (**tis-u = that**) the Almighty is not (**aavaee = come**) bestowed on* *him/her, (**ta**) then (**na key**) no one (**puchhai**) asks of (**vaat = state**) wellbeing, i.e. worldly status does not entitle one to receive honour of union with the Creator; deeds are considered for that.*

ਕੀਟਾ ਅੰਦਰਿ ਕੀਟੁ ਕਰਿ ਦੋਸੀ ਦੋਸੁ ਧਰੇ ॥
Kītā anḏar kīt kar ḏosī ḏos ḏẖare.

*A person who transgresses from Naam is (**kar-i = made**) treated as (**keett-u = a worm**) lowest (**andar-i**) amongst (**keetta = worms**) the lowly, i.e. faces ignominy; (**dosee**) the defaulter will be (**dharey = levied**) told of every (**dos-u**) fault of his/her - like other such souls and rejected for union with the Creator[1].*

ਨਾਨਕ ਨਿਰਗੁਣਿ ਗੁਣੁ ਕਰੇ ਗੁਣਵੰਤਿਆ ਗੁਣੁ ਦੇ ॥
Nānak nirguṇ guṇ kare guṇvanṯi▫ā guṇ ḏe.

---

1 ਜੇ ਕੋ ਨਾਉ ਧਰਾਏ ਵਡਾ ਸਾਦ ਕਰੇ ਮਨਿ ਭਾਣੇ ॥ ਖਸਮੈ ਨਦਰੀ ਕੀੜਾ ਆਵੈ ਜੇਤੇ ਚੁਗੈ ਦਾਣੇ ॥ ਮਰਿ ਮਰਿ ਜੀਵੈ ਤਾ ਕਿਛੁ ਪਾਏ ਨਾਨਕ ਨਾਮੁ ਵਖਾਣੇ ॥੩॥੫॥੩੯॥
Je ko nā▫o ḏẖarā▫e vadā sāḏ kare man bẖāṇe. Kẖasmai naḏrī kīṛā āvai jeṯe cẖugai ḏāṇe. Mar mar jīvai ṯā kicẖẖ pā▫e Nānak nām vakẖāṇe. ||3||5||39||

*(**Jey**) if (**ko**) someone (**dharaaey**) gets (**vaddaa**) a great (**naau**) name, i.e. becomes high and mighty, and (**karey = does, saad-u = taste**) acts (**man = by mind, bhaaney = liked**) as s/he likes.*
*But s/he (**aavai = comes, nadri = in sight**) is seen as (**keerra**) an insect (**khasmai**) by the Master; as s/he (**chugai**) pecks (**jetey**) all (**daaney**) grains, i.e. uses benedictions of the Almighty.*
*S/he can (**paaey**) receive (**kichh-u = some thing**) Divine grace only (**ta**) then if s/he (**jeevai**) lives (**mar-i mar-i = dying**) while giving up ego, and (**vakhaanai = utters**) remembers to live by (**naam-u**) Divine commands, says Nanak. 3. 5. 39. M: 1, p 360.*

The Almighty does not condemn any one permanently. *If one realizes his/her faults, then the Almighty leads the (**nirgun-i**) virtue-less person to the guru and (**karey = makes**) bestows (**gun-u**) the virtue – of complying with Naam; God (**dey = gives**) bestows more (**gun-u**) virtue of compliance with Naam, to (**gunvantiaa**) the virtuous*[1].

ਤੇਹਾ ਕੋਇ ਨ ਸੁਝਈ ਜਿ ਤਿਸੁ ਗੁਣੁ ਕੋਇ ਕਰੇ ॥੭॥
Ṫehā ko▫e na sujẖ▫ī jė ṯis guṇ ko▫e kare. ||7||

*There does not (**sujhaee**) seem to be (**teyha**) such a person (**j-i**) who can (**karey**) bestow (**koey**) any (**gun-u**) virtue to (**tis-u**) the Master – no one can be that wise as to advise the Almighty*[2]. *7.*

---

[1] Guru Nanak says:

ਗੁਣ ਸੰਗਿ ਰਹੰਸੀ ਖਰੀ ਸਰਸੀ ਜਾ ਰਾਵੀ ਰੰਗਿ ਰਾਤੈ ॥ ਅਵਗਣ ਮਾਰਿ ਗੁਣੀ ਘਰੁ ਛਾਇਆ ਪੂਰੈ ਪੁਰਖਿ ਬਿਧਾਤੈ ॥
Guṇ sang rahansī kẖarī sarsī jā rāvī rang rāṯai. Avgaṇ mār guṇī gẖar cẖẖā▫i▫ā pūrai purakẖ biḏẖāṯai.

*(**Ja**) when (**poorai**) the perfect (**purakh-i**) all-pervasive (**bidhaatai**) Creator (**rang-i = with love, raatai = imbued**) the loving Master, (**raavi = enjoyed, gave company**) is found within, the soul-wife (**rahansi**) is joyful (**sang-i = with**) seeing IT's (**gun**) virtues. (**Poorai**) the perfect (**purakh-i**) all-pervasive (**bidhaatai**) Creator (**maar-i = kills**) banishes (**avgan**) faults and (**chaaiaa = roofed**) fills (**guni**) with virtues. M: 1, p 764*

[2] This is because the Almighty is the highest

ਸਭ ਊਪਰਿ ਪਾਰਬ੍ਰਹਮੁ ਦਾਤਾਰੁ ॥ ਤੇਰੀ ਟੇਕ ਤੇਰਾ ਆਧਾਰੁ ॥ ਰਹਾਉ ॥
Sabẖ ūpar pārbarahm ḏāṯār. Ṫerī tek ṯerā āḏẖār. Rahā▫o.

Preface to Paurris 8-11.

Paurris 8 to 11 are on the subject of listening. They all end with the following statement, which is their underlying message:

ਨਾਨਕ ਭਗਤਾ ਸਦਾ ਵਿਗਾਸੁ ॥ ਸੁਣਿਐ ਦੂਖ ਪਾਪ ਕਾ ਨਾਸੁ ॥
Nānak bẖagṯā saḏā vigās. Suṇi▫ai ḏūkẖ pāp kā nās.

*Says Guru Nanak: (**Bhagta**) the devotees are (**sadaa**) ever (**vigaas-u = bloom**) joyful;*
*Because (**dookh**) faults and (**paap**) transgressions (**naas-u = destruction**) end (**suniai**) by listening to, and keeping Naam in mind; there then is no fear, apprehension of consequences or sense of guilt*[1].

---

*O (**paarbrahm-u = transcendent**) Supreme Being, You are (**daataar-u = giver of those who give**) the provider (**oopar-i**) above (**sabh**) all – others who may give do so after receiving from You; they have expectations in return for giving, but You have none.*
*The creatures exist with (**teyri**) Your (**tteyk**) support, i.e. ever look to You, and live with (**aadhaar-u = support**) the sustenance given by You.*
*(**Rahaau**) dwell on this and contemplate. M: 5, p 723.*

1 ਪਉੜੀ ॥ ਨਾਇ ਸੁਣਿਐ ਮਨੁ ਰਹਸੀਐ ਨਾਮੇ ਸਾਂਤਿ ਆਈ ॥ ਨਾਇ ਸੁਣਿਐ ਮਨੁ ਤ੍ਰਿਪਤੀਐ ਸਭ ਦੁਖ ਗਵਾਈ ॥
Pa▫oṛī. Nā▫e suṇi▫ai man rėhsī▫ai nāme sāʼnṯ ā▫ī. Nā▫e suṇi▫ai man ṯaripaṯ▫ī▫ai sabẖ ḏukẖ gavā▫ī.

*(**Paurri**) stanza by the fourth Guru. (**Suniai**) by listening to Naam – as present in our conscience and from wise people/in holy congregation, one does not digress and hence has no worries; (**man-u**) the mind (**rahaseeai**) remains in bliss; (**saant-i**) peace (**aai = comes**) is experienced with practice (**naamey**) of Naam.*

Paurri 8

ਸੁਣਿਐ ਸਿਧ ਪੀਰ ਸੁਰਿ ਨਾਥ ॥ ਸੁਣਿਐ ਧਰਤਿ ਧਵਲ ਆਕਾਸ ॥
Suṇi▫ai sidh pīr sur nāth. Suṇi▫ai dharat dhaval ākās.

*It is (**suniai**) by listening to the guru to understand Naam/Divine virtues and commands that –*

*One becomes aware that (**sidh**) accomplished saints, (**peer = Muslim expression for guru**) spiritual guides, (**sur-i**) god-like persons and (**naath – a clan of yogis**) yogis – all owe allegiance to the Almighty – as stated in Paurri 27 – gaavah-i sidh samddhi andar-i, i.e. in their meditation the saints praise the Almighty. One gets awareness that (**dharat-i**) the earth being held in space and (**dhaval = white bull**) the metaphoric bull supporting it, or (**aakaas**) the sky being like a canopy without support are metaphor, for the universe created and functioning by cosmic laws as shown in Paurri 16 below.*

ਸੁਣਿਐ ਦੀਪ ਲੋਅ ਪਾਤਾਲ ॥ ਸੁਣਿਐ ਪੋਹਿ ਨ ਸਕੈ ਕਾਲੁ ॥
Suṇi▫ai dīp lo▫a pātāl. Suṇi▫ai pohi na sakai kāl.

*One learns that Naam/cosmic laws apply in (**deep**) the islands in water, (**loa/lok**) land and (**paataal**) the lower regions[1].*

---

*The mind (**tripteeai = satiated**) feels satisfied (**suniai**) listening and practice (**naaey**) of Naam, as (**sabh**) all (**dukh**) grief/pain (**gavaai =lost**) goes. M: 4, p 1240.*

[1] The fourth Guru says:

ਧਰਤਿ ਪਾਤਾਲੁ ਆਕਾਸੁ ਹੈ ਮੇਰੀ ਜਿੰਦੁੜੀਏ ਸਭ ਹਰਿ ਹਰਿ ਨਾਮੁ ਧਿਆਵੈ ਰਾਮ ॥

*(**Kaal-u = agent of death**) the agent of Divine justice (**na sakai = cannot**) is not allowed to (**poh**) reach one who (**suniai**) listens to and obeys Naam, - the metaphoric Divine police has orders not to go near one who lives by Naam*[1]*.*

ਨਾਨਕ ਭਗਤਾ ਸਦਾ ਵਿਗਾਸੁ ॥ ਸੁਣਿਐ ਦੂਖ ਪਾਪ ਕਾ ਨਾਸੁ ॥
Nānak bẖagṯā saḏā vigās. Suṇi▫ai ḏūkẖ pāp kā nās. ||8||

*Says Guru Nanak: (**Bhagta**) the devotees are (**sadaa**) ever (**vigaas-u = bloom**) joyful;*
*Because (**dookh**) faults and (**paap**) transgressions (**naas-u = destruction**) end (**suniai**) by listening to, and keeping Naam in mind; there then is no fear, apprehension of consequences, or sense of guilt. 8.*

<u>Paurri 9</u>

ਸੁਣਿਐ ਈਸਰੁ ਬਰਮਾ ਇੰਦੁ ॥ Suṇi▫ai īsar barmā inḏ.
*It is (**suniai**) listening to the guru to understand Naam/Divine virtues and commands that –*

Ḏẖaraṯ pāṯāl ākās hai merī jinḏuṛī▫e sabẖ har har nām ḏẖi▫āvai rām.

*(**Dharat-i/dharti**) the earth, (**pataal-i**) nether regions and (**aakaas-u**) sky, (**sabh**) all (**dhiaavai = pay attention**) exist by, and obey, (**naam-u**) commands of the Almighty – the cosmic laws. M: 4, p 539.*

[1] ਸੁਣਿ ਸੁਣਿ ਇਹੁ ਮਨੁ ਨਿਰਮਲੁ ਹੋਵੈ ਕਟੀਐ ਕਾਲ ਕੀ ਫਾਸੀ ਰਾਮ ॥
Suṇ suṇ ih man nirmal hovai kaṯī▫ai kāl kī fāsī rām.

*(**Suni-i suni-i**) by ever listening to the myriad Divine virtues, (**ih = this**) the (**man-u**) mind (**nirmal-u hovai**) is cleansed of vices and (**phaasi**) the noose of (**kaal**) the agent of Divine justice (**katteeai**) is cut, i.e. one is no longer subject to punishment as one commits no vices. M: 5, p 781.*

We learn that the Hindu gods ***(eesar-u)*** *Mahadev/Shankar/Shiva, Brahma, and Indra – whom people worship – all act as commanded by the Almighty*[1]*.*

ਸੁਣਿਐ ਮੁਖਿ ਸਾਲਾਹਣ ਮੰਦੁ ॥
Suṇi▫ai mukẖ sālāhaṇ manḏ.

*(****Mand-u****) an evil person – who has turned away from God, starts (****salaahan****) praising (****mukh-i****) from the mouth, and obeying, the Almighty*[2]*.*

ਸੁਣਿਐ ਜੋਗ ਜੁਗਤਿ ਤਨਿ ਭੇਦ ॥ ਸੁਣਿਐ ਸਾਸਤ ਸਿਮ੍ਰਿਤਿ ਵੇਦ ॥
Suṇi▫ai jog jugaṯ ṯan bẖeḏ. Suṇi▫ai sāsaṯ simriṯ veḏ.

*It is (****suniai****) listening to the guru to understand Naam/Divine virtues and commands that –*

---

[1] ਈਸਰੁ ਬ੍ਰਹਮਾ ਦੇਵੀ ਦੇਵਾ ॥ ਇੰਦ੍ਰ ਤਪੇ ਮੁਨਿ ਤੇਰੀ ਸੇਵਾ ॥
Īsar barahmā ḏevī ḏevā. Inḏar ṯape mun ṯerī sevā. Jaṯī saṯī keṯe banvāsī anṯ na ko▫ī pā▫iḏā. ||3||

*(****Eesar-u****) Shankar/Mahadev, Brahma, (****deyvi****) goddesses, (****deyva****) gods; Indra, (****tapey****) austere ascetics and (****mun-i****) sages are in (****teyri****) Your (****seyva****) service, i.e. obey You. M: 1, p 1034.*

[2] ਸੁਣਤੇ ਪੁਨੀਤ ਕਹਤੇ ਪਵਿਤੁ ਸਤਿਗੁਰੁ ਰਹਿਆ ਭਰਪੂਰੇ ॥
Suṇṯe punīṯ kahṯe paviṯ saṯgur rahi▫ā bẖarpūre.

*Those who (****suntey****) listen are (****puneet****) purified of vices and those who (****kahtey = say****) propagate it are also (****pavit-u/pavitr****) purified as they find (****satigur-u****) the true guru (****rahiaa bharpoorey****) present – and act on his teachings, wherever they are. M: 3, p 922, Anand Sahib.*

*We learn about (**bheyd**) the mysteries (**tan-i**) of the body, i.e. how mind works and tempted away from God; and (**jugat = method**) how to attain (**jog**) union with the Almighty[1].*
*We learn about how Smritis, Shastras and (**veyd**) Vedas talk of Maaiaa, and that compliance of Naam saves from those.*

ਨਾਨਕ ਭਗਤਾ ਸਦਾ ਵਿਗਾਸੁ ॥ ਸੁਣਿਐ ਦੂਖ ਪਾਪ ਕਾ ਨਾਸੁ ॥
Nānak bẖagṯā saḏā vigās. Suṇi▫ai ḏūkẖ pāp kā nās. ||9||

*Says Guru Nanak: (**Bhagta**) the devotees are (**sadaa**) ever (**vigaas-u = bloom**) joyful;*
*Because (**dookh**) faults and (**paap**) transgressions (**naas-u = destruction**) end (**suniai**) by listening to, and keeping Naam in mind; there then is no fear, apprehension of consequences, or sense of guilt. 9.*

Paurri 10

ਸੁਣਿਐ ਸਤੁ ਸੰਤੋਖੁ ਗਿਆਨੁ ॥ ਸੁਣਿਐ ਅਠਸਠਿ ਕਾ ਇਸਨਾਨੁ ॥
Suṇi▫ai saṯ sanṯokẖ gi▫ān. uṇi▫ai aṯẖsaṯẖ kā isnān

*It is (**suniai**) by listening to the guru to understand Naam/Divine virtues and commands that –*

---

[1] ਜੋਗ ਜੁਗਤਿ ਸੁਨਿ ਆਇਓ ਗੁਰ ਤੇ ॥ ਮੋ ਕਉ ਸਤਿਗੁਰ ਸਬਦਿ ਬੁਝਾਇਓ ॥੧॥ ਰਹਾਉ ॥
Jog jugaṯ sun ā▫i▫o gur ṯe. Mo ka▫o saṯgur sabaḏ bujẖā▫i▫o. ||1|| rahā▫o.

*I have (**aaio**) come back after (**sun-i**) listening (**tey**) from (**gur**) the guru (jugat-i) the method of attaining (**jog**) union with the Almighty.*
*The (**satgur**) true guru gave (**mo kau = to me**) me (**bujhaaio**) understanding (**sabad-i = of the word**) of Naam/Divine commands. 1. M: 5, p 208.*

*We (**giaan-u**) learn to live (**sat-u**) truthfully and be (**santokh-u** = **contentment**) happy with Divine will*[1].

*The mind is purified, for which people go and take (**isnaan-u**) bath (**ka**) of (**atthsatth-i**) sixtyeight places of pilgrimage. This is elucidated by Paurri 20 saying* "Bhareeai mat-i paapa kai sang-i; oh-u dhopai navai kai rang-i" *the mind defiled by transgressions is purified with love of Naam.*

ਸੁਣਿਐ ਪੜਿ ਪੜਿ ਪਾਵਹਿ ਮਾਨੁ ॥ ਸੁਣਿਐ ਲਾਗੈ ਸਹਜਿ ਧਿਆਨੁ ॥

Suṇiªai paṛ paṛ pāvahi mān. Suṇiªai lāgai sahj ḏẖiªān.

*One obtains awareness about right conduct and (**paavah-i**) obtain (**maan**) recognition for which people (**parr-i parr-i**) read scriptures - but engage in arguments to get recognition.*

*(**Dhiaan-u**) concentration of the mind is (**sahj-i**) effortlessly (**laagai**) attained.*

ਨਾਨਕ ਭਗਤਾ ਸਦਾ ਵਿਗਾਸੁ ॥ ਸੁਣਿਐ ਦੂਖ ਪਾਪ ਕਾ ਨਾਸੁ ॥

---

[1] Guru Nanak says in Sidh Gostt:

ਗੁਰਮੁਖਿ ਨਾਮੁ ਦਾਨੁ ਇਸਨਾਨੁ ॥ ਗੁਰਮੁਖਿ ਲਾਗੈ ਸਹਜਿ ਧਿਆਨੁ ॥

Gurmukẖ nām ḏān isnān. Gurmukẖ lāgai sahj ḏẖiªān.

*(**Gurmukh-i**) one who follows the guru's guidance, lives by (**naam-u**) Divine virtues and commands, s/he (**daan-u** = **charity**) shares with others and (**isnaan-u**) bathes in, i.e. purifies the self, with Naam.*

*By following the guru's teachings (**dhiaan-u**) attention (**laagai**) remains fixed on Naam (**sahj-i**) with poise. M: 1, p 942.*

Nānak bẖagṯā saḏā vigās. Suṇi▫ai ḏūkẖ pāp kā nās. ||10||

*Says Guru Nanak: (**Bhagta**) the devotees are (**sadaa**) ever (**vigaas-u = bloom**) joyful;*
*Because (**dookh**) faults and (**paap**) transgressions (**naas-u = destruction**) end (**suniai**) by listening to, and keeping Naam in mind; there then is no fear, apprehension of consequences, or sense of guilt. 10.*

Paurri 11

ਸੁਣਿਐ ਸਰਾ ਗੁਣਾ ਕੇ ਗਾਹ ॥ ਸੁਣਿਐ ਸੇਖ ਪੀਰ ਪਾਤਿਸਾਹ ॥
Suṇi▫ai sarā guṇā ke gāh. Suṇi▫ai sekẖ pīr pāṯisāh.

ਸੁਣਿਐ ਅੰਧੇ ਪਾਵਹਿ ਰਾਹੁ ॥ ਸੁਣਿਐ ਹਾਥ ਹੋਵੈ ਅਸਗਾਹੁ ॥
Suṇi▫ai anḏẖe pāvahi rāhu. Suṇi▫ai hāth hovai asgāhu.

*It is (**suniai**) listening to the guru to understand Naam/Divine virtues and commands that –*

*One is able to (**gaah**) wade through (**saraa**) oceans of (**gunaa**) virtues, i.e. get hard-to-obtain awareness of virtues.*
*One gets awareness that (**seykh**) Sheikhs – Muslim person holding spiritual and temporal authority, (**peer**) preceptors and (**paatsaah**) emperors are subject to Divine commands.*
*(**Andhey**) blind persons (**paavah-i**) find (**raah-u**) the path, i.e. ignorant persons are enlightened on how to lead life.*
*(**Asgaah-u**) bottomless ocean (**hovai**) comes in (**haath**) hand, i.e. one is able get across/overcome the world ocean of temptations and unite with the Almighty.*

ਨਾਨਕ ਭਗਤਾ ਸਦਾ ਵਿਗਾਸੁ ॥ ਸੁਣਿਐ ਦੂਖ ਪਾਪ ਕਾ ਨਾਸੁ ॥

Nānak bẖagṯā saḏā vigās. Suṇiai ḏūkẖ pāp kā nās. ||11||

*Says Guru Nanak: (**Bhagta**) the devotees are (**sadaa**) ever (**vigaas-u = bloom**) joyful;*
*Because (**dookh**) faults and (**paap**) transgressions (**naas-u = destruction**) end (**suniai**) by listening to, and keeping Naam in mind; there then is no fear, apprehension of consequences, or sense of guilt. 11.*

As may be seen, listening – obtaining awareness/knowledge brings happiness. The Guru restates this in Paurri 36 after describing Giaan Khandd, the realm of knowledge in Paurri 35 thus:

ਗਿਆਨ ਖੰਡ ਮਹਿ ਗਿਆਨੁ ਪਰਚੰਡੁ ॥ ਤਿਥੈ ਨਾਦ ਬਿਨੋਦ ਕੋਡ ਅਨੰਦੁ ॥
Giān kẖand mėh giān parcẖand. Ŧithai nāḏ binoḏ kod anand.

Knowledge reigns supreme in the realm of learning;
One enjoys the celestial music and great bliss. Paurri 36.

This confirms the underlying message of Pauris 8-11 given above, because listening is learning.

The Guru has thus introduced the principle that awareness of Naam is necessary in order to avoid the pitfalls that we face in life all the time. One who does that leads a life in bliss[1].

---

[1] ਨਾਮੁ ਸੁਣੀਐ ਨਾਮੁ ਮੰਨੀਐ ਨਾਮੇ ਵਡਿਆਈ ॥ਨਾਮੁ ਸਲਾਹੇ ਸਦਾ ਸਦਾ ਨਾਮੇ ਮਹਲੁ ਪਾਈ ॥੪॥
Nām suṇīai nām mannīai nāme vadiāī. Nām salāhe saḏā saḏā nāme mahal pāī. ||4||

*We should (**suniai**) listen to and (**manniai**) obey Naam; one obtains (**vadiaaee**) glory (**naamey**) by obedience to Naam.*

Suniai/listening is meant for compliance. It is significant that Paurris 12-15 which are on compliance/obedience follow Paurris 8-11 which are about listening or learning.

Preface to Paurris 12-15 (Ma'nney/Ma'nnai)

Japji includes the subject of Manney/Mannai i.e. believing and obeying at three places; in Paurris/stanzas 12-15, in Paurri 36 (Saram khandd) and the Slok/epilogue.

The last two lines of each of Paurris 12-15 end with the following underlying message:

ਐਸਾ ਨਾਮੁ ਨਿਰੰਜਨੁ ਹੋਇ ॥ ਜੇ ਕੋ ਮੰਨਿ ਜਾਣੈ ਮਨਿ ਕੋਇ ॥
Aisā nām niranjan ho▫e. Je ko man jāṇai man ko▫e. ||

*(**Aisa**) such is (**niranjan-u** = **unstained**) the purifying Naam; only (**jey**) if (**ko**) someone (**mann-i**) obeys; (**koey**) some rare person truly obeys and (**jaanai** = **knows**) experiences that – freedom from influence of temptations - (**man-i**) in mind.*

Out of these four Paurris, Paurri 12 is about the state attained by ਮੰਨੇ/Ma'nney i.e. obedience, while Paurris 13-15 describe what is achieved by one who ਮੰਨੈ/Mannai, i.e. obeys.

Paurri 12

ਮੰਨੇ ਕੀ ਗਤਿ ਕਹੀ ਨ ਜਾਇ ॥ ਜੇ ਕੋ ਕਹੈ ਪਿਛੈ ਪਛੁਤਾਇ ॥

---

*One who (**sadaa sadaa**) forever (**salaahey**) praises and lives by Naam, s/he (**paaee** = **finds**) gets to (**mahal-u** = **palace**) the Almighty (naamey) through living by Naam. 4.* M: 3, p 426.

Manne kī gaṯ kahī na jā▫e. Je ko kahai picẖẖai pacẖẖuṯā▫e.

(Gat-i = state) *the state of – freedom from temptations that is attained by* ***(manney)*** *obeying Naam* ***(na jaaey)*** *cannot be* ***(kahee)*** *told – it can only be experienced.*
(Jey) *if* ***(ko)*** *someone* ***(kahai)*** *says – that s/he knows – then s/he* ***(pachhutaaey)*** *repents* ***(pichhai)*** *later*[1].

Message: There are people who claim have clean minds free of vices so they need not worry about Naam. They act by ego/self-will, go astray, suffer and then realise their folly.

ਕਾਗਦਿ ਕਲਮ ਨ ਲਿਖਣਹਾਰੁ ॥ ਮੰਨੇ ਕਾ ਬਹਿ ਕਰਨਿ ਵੀਚਾਰੁ ॥

---

[1] Paurri 36 which deals with *Saram Khand*, the realm of endeavour/obedience, uses almost the same words as in Paurris 12 to describe this as molding the self:

ਸਰਮ ਖੰਡ ਕੀ ਬਾਣੀ ਰੂਪੁ ॥ ਤਿਥੈ ਘਾੜਤਿ ਘੜੀਐ ਬਹੁਤੁ ਅਨੂਪੁ ॥
ਤਾ ਕੀਆ ਗਲਾ ਕਥੀਆ ਨਾ ਜਾਹਿ ॥ ਜੇ ਕੋ ਕਹੈ ਪਿਛੈ ਪਛੁਤਾਇ ॥
Saram kẖand kī baṇī rūp. Ŧithai gẖāṛaṯ gẖaṛī▫ai bahuṯ anūp.
Ŧā kī▫ā galā kathī▫ā nā jāhi. Je ko kahai picẖẖai pacẖẖuṯā▫e.

(Baani/bantar) *construction/state of* ***(khandd)*** *the realm of* ***(saram)*** *effort/obedience is* ***(roop-u)*** *good looks.*
(Tithai) *there the mind* ***(gharreeai)*** *is shaped with* ***(ghaarrat-i = carving)*** *shape of* ***(bahut-u)*** *very* ***(anoop-u)*** *incomparable beauty* ***(gharreeai)*** *is carved, i.e. the mind is different from ordinary minds which succumb to temptations/other ideas, i.e. the most sublime state of freedom from temptations is attained.*
(Galaa = things) *the experience* ***(ki)*** *of* ***(ta)*** *that mind* ***(na jaaey)*** *cannot be* ***(katheeaa)*** *stated;* ***(jey)*** *if* ***(ko)*** *someone* ***(kahai = says)*** *describes, s/he* ***(pachhutaaey)*** *repents* ***(pichhai)*** *later.*

Kāgaḏ kalam na likẖaṇhār. Manne kā bahi karan vīcẖār.

*There is no (**likhahaar-u**) writer and no (**kalam**) pen capable of writing this experience (**kaagad-i**) on paper, i.e. this state is beyond description.*
*The seekers (**bah-i**) sit together and (**karan-i = do, veechaar-u = reflection**) exchange their experiences.*

ਐਸਾ ਨਾਮੁ ਨਿਰੰਜਨੁ ਹੋਇ ॥ ਜੇ ਕੋ ਮੰਨਿ ਜਾਣੈ ਮਨਿ ਕੋਇ ॥੧੨॥
Aisā nām niranjan ho▫e. Je ko man jāṇai man ko▫e. ||12||

*(**Aisa**) such is (**niranjan-u = unstained**) the purifying Naam; only (**jey**) if (**ko**) someone (**mann-i**) obeys; but (**koey**) some rare person truly obeys and (**jaanai = knows**) experiences that – freedom from influence of temptations - (**man-i**) in mind. 12.*

Paurri 13

ਮੰਨੈ ਸੁਰਤਿ ਹੋਵੈ ਮਨਿ ਬੁਧਿ ॥ ਮੰਨੈ ਸਗਲ ਭਵਣ ਕੀ ਸੁਧਿ ॥ ਮੰਨੈ ਮੁਹਿ ਚੋਟਾ ਨਾ ਖਾਇ ॥ ਮੰਨੈ ਜਮ ਕੈ ਸਾਥਿ ਨ ਜਾਇ ॥
Mannai suraṯ hovai man buḏẖ. Mannai sagal bẖavaṇ kī suḏẖ. Mannai muhi cẖotā nā kẖā▫e. Mannai jam kai sāth na jā▫e.

Translation of the above lines available on internet is as follows.

"By truly believing in the Lord's Name Divine comprehension enters man's mind and understanding. By truly believing in God's Name the Knowledge of all the spheres is acquired.
The worshipper of God suffers not blows on his face. Through inner belief in the Lord's Name man goes not with death's minister".

It would be noticed that the first two lines in the above translation mention acquiring the understanding, while the latter two indicate achievement as both are on Ma'nnai – by obedience. The first two lines should also indicate compliance.

This dichotomy is removed by understanding Paurri 36, which describes Saram Khandd the realm of endeavour/action[1]. Interpretation of Paurri 13 and Paurri 36 should accord. The first two lines of Paurri 13 may therefore be interpreted thus:

ਮੰਨੈ ਸੁਰਤਿ ਹੋਵੈ ਮਨਿ ਬੁਧਿ ॥ ਮੰਨੈ ਸਗਲ ਭਵਣ ਕੀ ਸੁਧਿ ॥ ਮੰਨੈ ਮੁਹਿ ਚੋਟਾ ਨਾ ਖਾਇ ॥ ਮੰਨੈ ਜਮ ਕੈ ਸਾਥਿ ਨ ਜਾਇ ॥
Mannai suraṯ hovai man buḏẖ. Mannai sagal bẖavaṇ kī suḏẖ. Mannai muhi cẖotā nā kẖā▫e. Mannai jam kai sāth na jā▫e.

By believing/obedience -
*(**Surat-i**) consciousness and (**budh-i**) understanding (**man-i**) of the mind (**hovai = happens**) becomes, i.e. is transformed and one does not stray.*

---

[1] ਤਿਥੈ ਘੜੀਐ ਸੁਰਤਿ ਮਤਿ ਮਨਿ ਬੁਧਿ ॥ ਤਿਥੈ ਘੜੀਐ ਸੁਰਾ ਸਿਧਾ ਕੀ ਸੁਧਿ ॥੩੬॥
Ŧithai gẖaṛī▫ai suraṯ maṯ man buḏẖ. Ŧithai gẖaṛī▫ai surā siḏẖā kī suḏẖ. ||36||

*(**Tithai**) there the mind (**surat-i**) consciousness, (**mat-i**) thinking faculty (**man-i**) of the mind and (**budh-i**) intellect (**gharreeai**) are carved/shaped.*
*(**Tithai**) there, (**sudh-i**) awareness of (**suraa**) gods and (**sidhaa**) accomplished saints, i.e. those who experience God's presence -, (**gharreeai = carved**) is transformed. 36.*

*(**Sudh-i**) awareness – that God and Naam/Divine commands is present – in (**sagal**) all (**bhavan**) places is obtained.*
*One – commits no transgressions and thus - does not (**khaaey = eat/bear**) receive (**chotta**) hits (**muh-i**) on the face, i.e. is not subjected to indignities as a result.*
*One who (**ma'nnai**) obeys Naam does not (**jaaey**) go (**saath-i**) with, i.e. is not sent for rebirth by, (**jam**) Divine justice – but honourably unites with the Almighty.*

ਐਸਾ ਨਾਮੁ ਨਿਰੰਜਨੁ ਹੋਇ ॥ ਜੇ ਕੋ ਮੰਨਿ ਜਾਣੈ ਮਨਿ ਕੋਇ ॥੧੩॥
Aisā nām niranjan ho▫e. Je ko man jāṇai man ko▫e. ||13||

*(**Aisa**) such is (**niranjan-u = unstained**) the purifying Naam; only (**jey**) if (**ko**) someone (**mann-i**) obeys; but (**koey**) some rare person truly obeys and (**jaanai = knows**) experiences that – freedom from influence of temptations - (**man-i**) in mind. 13.*

Paurri 14

ਮੰਨੈ ਮਾਰਗਿ ਠਾਕ ਨ ਪਾਇ ॥ ਮੰਨੈ ਪਤਿ ਸਿਉ ਪਰਗਟੁ ਜਾਇ ॥ ਮੰਨੈ ਮਗੁ ਨ ਚਲੈ ਪੰਥੁ ॥ ਮੰਨੈ ਧਰਮ ਸੇਤੀ ਸਨਬੰਧੁ ॥
Mannai mārag ṯẖāk na pā▫e. Mannai paṯ si▫o pargat jā▫e. Mannai mag na cẖalai panth. Mannai ḏẖaram seṯī san▫banḏẖ.

One who obeys Naam:

*(**Paaey = receive**) faces no (**tthaak**) obstacles*

*(**maarag-i**) on path to God, i.e. the obstacle of Haumai/ego is dissolved.*
*S/he (**jaaey**) goes to, and (**pargatt-u = manifest**) received by, God (**siau**) with (**pat-i**) honour;*

*Does not to (**chalai**) walk on any other (**mag-u = path, panth-u = path**) path, - than obedience to Naam, i.e. s/he does stray.*
*For, s/he has (**sanbandh-u = relationship**) connection (**dharam**) dutifulness, i.e. has Naam in mind and other ideas driven away.*

ਐਸਾ ਨਾਮੁ ਨਿਰੰਜਨੁ ਹੋਇ ॥ ਜੇ ਕੋ ਮੰਨਿ ਜਾਣੈ ਮਨਿ ਕੋਇ ॥੧੪॥
Aisā nām niranjan ho▫e. Je ko man jāṇai man ko▫e. ||14||

*(**Aisa**) such is (**niranjan-u = unstained**) the purifying Naam; only (**jey**) if (**ko**) someone (**mann-i**) obeys; but (**koey**) some rare person truly obeys and (**jaanai = knows**) experiences that – freedom from influence of temptations - (**man-i**) in mind. 14.*

Paurri 15
ਮੰਨੈ ਪਾਵਹਿ ਮੋਖੁ ਦੁਆਰੁ ॥ ਮੰਨੈ ਪਰਵਾਰੈ ਸਾਧਾਰੁ ॥ ਮੰਨੈ ਤਰੈ ਤਾਰੇ ਗੁਰੁ ਸਿਖ ॥ ਮੰਨੈ ਨਾਨਕ ਭਵਹਿ ਨ ਭਿਖ ॥
Mannai pāvahi mokẖḏu▫ār. Mannai parvārai sāḏẖār. Mannai ṯarai ṯāre gur sikẖ. Mannai Nānak bẖavahi na bẖikẖ.

*(**Mannai**) by obedience, one -*
*(**paavah-i**) gets (**mokh-u**) emancipation, i.e. liberation from temptations, and entry to (**duaar-u = gate**) the Divine abode/union with the Almighty.*
*And, is (**saadhaar-u**) good support (**parvaarai**) for the family, i.e. is a good householder.*
*Such a person is (**gur-u**) the guru who (**tarai = swims**) gets across the world-ocean and (**taarai**) ferries (**sikh**) the disciples with him.*
*S/he focuses on obedience of the One Almighty and does not (**bhavah-i**) wander seeking (**bhikh**) alms, i.e. looking elsewhere, says Guru Nanak.*

Note: Paurri 4 said “Nadri mokh-u duaar-u” liberation from temptations and entry to God’s abode is obtained with Divine grace. Now Paurri 15 says “mannai paavai mokh-u duaar-u” it is by obedience that the above is obtained. So one obtains union with the Almighty, and liberation from cycles of births and deaths after death, by Divine grace - which in turn is received by obedience to the Almighty.

ਐਸਾ ਨਾਮੁ ਨਿਰੰਜਨੁ ਹੋਇ ॥ ਜੇ ਕੋ ਮੰਨਿ ਜਾਣੈ ਮਨਿ ਕੋਇ ॥੧੫॥
Aisā nām niranjan ho▫e. Je ko man jāṇai man ko▫e. ||15||

*(**Aisa**) such is (**niranjan-u = unstained**) the purifying Naam; only (**jey**) if (**ko**) someone (**mann-i**) obeys; but (**koey**) some rare person truly obeys and (**jaanai = knows**) experiences that – freedom from influence of temptations - (**man-i**) in mind. 15.*

Preface to Pauris 16 to 19

Paurris 16 to 19 describe the process of creation, and its diversity. All components of creation exist and function together in harmony according to cosmic laws, which are unchanging. Paurri 16 has three parts.

Paurri 16 Part 1

The first starts with the term ਪੰਚ ਪਰਵਾਣ meaning the Panch are accepted/approved by the Almighty. In South Asia, the term ‘Panch’ is used for member/members of a village council called Panchayat and shows recognition as leaders. It has been variously interpreted as follows in context of Paurri 16 as follows:

1. Panch also means the count of five. Those who practice the five things mentioned earlier in Japji Sahib:

Hukam rajaaee chalna – are happy with Divine will, Gaaveeai – sing/praise God, suniaa – listen to Naam, Ma'nniaa = obey Naam, Rakheeai bhaau – keep Naam lovingly in mind – Bhai Vir Singh.

2. Those who remain absorbed in God; they become leaders – Prof Sahib Singh.

3. Those above Parpanch/machinations of the world – Giaani Harbans Singh.

4. The chosen ones – Dr Sant Singh Khalsa.

5. The elect – Bhai Manmohan Singh.

Paurri 35 below[1] elucidates Panch. It applies

---

[1] Paurri 35 says: ਕਰਮੀ ਕਰਮੀ ਹੋਇ ਵੀਚਾਰੁ ॥ ਸਚਾ ਆਪਿ ਸਚਾ ਦਰਬਾਰੁ ॥ Karmī karmī ho▫e vīcẖār. Sacẖā āp sacẖā ḏarbār.

*(**Karmi karmi**) deeds of all creatures (**hoey = is done, veechaar-u = consideration**) are considered. (**Aap-i = self**) the Creator is (**sachaa = true**) just and the Divine (**darbaar-u**) court is (**sachaa**) just, i.e. everyone's deeds are evaluated without prejudice, in other words everything happens logically and naturally.*

ਤਿਥੈ ਸੋਹਨਿ ਪੰਚ ਪਰਵਾਣੁ ॥ ਨਦਰੀ ਕਰਮਿ ਪਵੈ ਨੀਸਾਣੁ ॥
Ŧithai sohan pancẖ parvāṇ. Naḏrī karam pavai nīsāṇ.

*(**Tithai**) there, in Divine court (**panch**) those who live by Divine commands (**sohan-i = look good**) are glorified and (**parvaan-u**) accepted for union by the Creator.*
*(**Neesaan-u**) the sign of acceptance (**pavai = is put**) is marked on them (**nadri karam-i**) by Divine grace.*
So the Panch are those who act by Divine virtues and commands.

to those who are approved based on deeds, i.e. those who live by Naam/Divine commands.

ਪੰਚ ਪਰਵਾਣ ਪੰਚ ਪਰਧਾਨੁ ॥ ਪੰਚੇ ਪਾਵਹਿ ਦਰਗਹਿ ਮਾਨੁ ॥

Panch̲ parvāṇ panch̲ pard̲h̲ān. Panch̲ parvāṇ panch̲ par d̲h̲ān.

*The Panch, those who obey Divine commands/natural laws, are (**parvaan**) accepted/approved of by people; a Panch becomes (**pardhaan-u = president**) a leader, i.e. receives recognition in the world.*
*(**Panchey**) the Panch do not transgress and - (**paavah-i**) receive (**maan-u**) honour (**dargah-i**) in Divine court, i.e. honourably unite with God.*

ਪੰਚੇ ਸੋਹਹਿ ਦਰਿ ਰਾਜਾਨੁ ॥ ਪੰਚਾ ਕਾ ਗੁਰੁ ਏਕੁ ਧਿਆਨੁ ॥

Panch̲e pāvahi d̲argahi mān. Panch̲e sohahi d̲ar rājān.

*The Panch (**sohah-i = look good**) are glorified (**dar-i**) in court (**raajaan-u = king**) of the Sovereign Almighty – by way of acceptance for union with the Creator.*
*The Panch are those who fix (**eyk-u = one**) single-minded (**dhiaan-u**) attention on teachings of (**gur-u**) the guru – who teaches to comply with Naam/Divine commands.*

Paurri 16 Part 2

ਜੇ ਕੋ ਕਹੈ ਕਰੈ ਵੀਚਾਰੁ ॥ ਕਰਤੇ ਕੈ ਕਰਣੈ ਨਾਹੀ ਸੁਮਾਰੁ ॥

Je ko kahai karai vīch̲ār. Kart̲e kai karṇai nāhī sumār.

*(**Jey**) if (**ko**) someone (**kahai**) says that s/he knows the Creator's powers, then s/he (**karai = does, veechaar-u = reflection**) should reflect and would realize that (**sumaar-u**) estimation/measure of*

*(**karnai = doings**) creation (**kai**) of (**kartey**) the Creator is (**naahi**) not possible.*

This is how. There is an old Indian belief that a white bull supports the earth. Similarly, the Greek believe that Atlas supports the heavens. Guru Nanak takes note of this and says that the bull is a myth; the earth and other planets are held in space according to cosmic laws - like the string controls beads of a rosary.

ਧੌਲੁ ਧਰਮੁ ਦਇਆ ਕਾ ਪੂਤੁ ॥ ਸੰਤੋਖੁ ਥਾਪਿ ਰਖਿਆ ਜਿਨਿ ਸੂਤਿ ॥
Ḏẖoul ḏẖaram ḏa▫i▫ā kā pūṯ. Santoḵẖ thāp rakẖi▫ā jin sūṯ.

*The metaphoric (**dhoul-u**) white bull represents (**dharam-u**) the Divine law (**poot-u**) son (**ka**) of (**daiaa**) compassion, i.e. the Creator is kind to support the planets in space, by making cosmic laws, (**jin-i**) which (**rakhiaa**) keep every component of creation (**santokh-u = contented**) obediently (**soot-i = by the thread – like that in a rosary**) in their allotted positions.*

ਜੇ ਕੋ ਬੁਝੈ ਹੋਵੈ ਸਚਿਆਰੁ ॥ ਧਵਲੈ ਉਪਰਿ ਕੇਤਾ ਭਾਰੁ ॥
Je ko bujẖai hovai sacẖiār. Ḏẖavlai upar keṯā bẖār.

*(**Jey**) if someone (**bujhai**) understands and (**hovai = is, sachiaar-u = is truthful**) knows the truth. Then s/he should tell (**keyta**) how much (**bhaar-u**) load can there be (**upar-i**) on (**dhavlai**) the bull, i.e. how much weight a bull can bear?*

ਧਰਤੀ ਹੋਰੁ ਪਰੈ ਹੋਰੁ ਹੋਰੁ ॥ ਤਿਸ ਤੇ ਭਾਰੁ ਤਲੈ ਕਵਣੁ ਜੋਰੁ ॥
Ḏẖarṯī hor parai hor hor. Ŧis ṯe bẖār ṯalai kavaṇ jor.

*In addition, there are (**dhartee = earth**) planets (**parai**) beyond (**dhartee**) the earth and (**hor-u**) further away from the earth and (**hor-u**) farther away.*
*(**Kavan-u**) what is (**jor-u = strength**) the support (**talai**) under (**tis**) their (**bhaar-u**) load/weight?*

These two verses have also been interpreted to say that if the bull supports the earth, it must itself be supported by something and that something by another something. What are those supports? Either way the concept of the bull supporting the earth is hard to explain. Further -

ਜੀਅ ਜਾਤਿ ਰੰਗਾ ਕੇ ਨਾਵ ॥ ਸਭਨਾ ਲਿਖਿਆ ਵੁੜੀ ਕਲਾਮ ॥
Jī▫a jāṯ rangā ke nāv. Sabẖnā likẖi▫ā vuṛī kalām.

*There are (**jeea**) creatures (**key**) of numerous (**jaat-i**) types, (**rangaa**) hues and (**naav**) names/attributes/roles. The Creator's (**kalaam**) pen (**vurree**) moved and (**likhiaa = written**) wrote/allotted roles/made the laws for the role of (**sabhna = all**) each of them*[1].

ਏਹੁ ਲੇਖਾ ਲਿਖਿ ਜਾਣੈ ਕੋਇ ॥ ਲੇਖਾ ਲਿਖਿਆ ਕੇਤਾ ਹੋਇ ॥
Ėhu lekẖā likẖ jāṇai ko▫e. Lekẖā likẖi▫ā keṯā ho▫e.

*If (**koey**) someone (**jaanai**) knows how to (**likh-i**) write (**leykha = writing**) laws; then (**keyta**) how much (**leykha**) writing there (**hoey**) would be, i.e. no one knows expanse/roles laws of the entire creation.*

---

[1] This is stated again in Paurri 19 as "jeyta keeta teyta teyta naau" all those created have commands/laws for them; and Paurri 34 "Tis vich-u jeea jugat-i key rang; tin key naam aneyk anant" the world has creatures of different types and hues to whom numerous orders/laws apply.

ਕੇਤਾ ਤਾਣੁ ਸੁਆਲਿਹੁ ਰੂਪੁ ॥ ਕੇਤੀ ਦਾਤਿ ਜਾਣੈ ਕੌਣੁ ਕੂਤੁ ॥
Keṯā ṯāṇ su▫ālihu rūp. Keṯī ḏāṯ jāṇai kouṇ kūṯ.

*(**Keyta**) how vast are (**taan-u**) powers/domain of the Creator, and how (**suaalih-u**) beautiful (**roop-u = form**) the creation is; who can knows all this?*
*(**Keyti**) how many (**daat-i**) benedictions the Creator has bestowed, i.e. what all the Creator has provided in the form of food, fruits, air, water, milk, day, night, limbs, intellect etc. (**Koun-u**) who (**jaanai**) knows (**koot-u = estimation**) the count of all these.*

These are difficult to fathom.

Note: The Old Testament, the common scripture of the Jews, Christians and Muslims, which says God created the earth, its sky and what exists on them, in six days. Probably taking note of this, Guru Nanak says:

ਕੀਤਾ ਪਸਾਉ ਏਕੋ ਕਵਾਉ ॥ ਤਿਸ ਤੇ ਹੋਏ ਲਖ ਦਰੀਆਉ ॥
Kīṯā pasā▫o eko kavā▫o. Ŧis ṯe ho▫e lakẖ ḏarī▫ā▫o.

*The Creator (**keeta = made, pasaau = expansion**) from a core with (**eyko**) with one (**kuvaau**) command.*
*Lakhs of (**dareeaau**) streams/branches (**hoey = happened**) flowed (**tey**) from (**tis**) that[1].*

---

[1] This is verified by the fifth Guru thus:

ਵਣੁ ਤ੍ਰਿਣੁ ਤ੍ਰਿਭਵਣ ਪਾਣੀ ॥ ਚਾਰਿ ਬੇਦ ਚਾਰੇ ਖਾਣੀ ॥ ਖੰਡ ਦੀਪ ਸਭਿ ਲੋਆ ॥ ਏਕ ਕਵਾਵੈ ਤੇ ਸਭਿ ਹੋਆ ॥੧॥

vaṇ ṯariṇ ṯaribẖavaṇ pāṇī. Cẖār beḏ cẖāre kẖāṇī. Kẖand ḏīp sabẖ lo▫ā. Ėk kavāvai ṯe sabẖ ho▫ā. ||1||

Note: Guru Nanak made the above statement in the fifteen or early sixteenth century CE. The Big Bang theory enunciated by Georges LeMaitre in 1927 and Edwin Hubble in 1929 is on the same lines.

Paurri 16 Part 3, and Paurris 17-19

ਕੁਦਰਤਿ ਕਵਣ ਕਹਾ ਵੀਚਾਰੁ ॥

Kuḏraṯ kavaṇ kahā vīcẖār.

*(**Kavan**) what (**veechaar-u**) view can I (**kahaa** = **say**) express on Your (**kaudrat-i**) powers, o Creator.*

Note: Paurri 16 has mentioned the greatness and infinite nature of the Creator and the creation saying these are beyond human estimate/comprehension. The succeeding Paurris elaborate this as follows:

1. Paurris 16, 17, 19. **Kudrat-i kavan kahaa** veechaar – the Creator's powers cannot be stated; we should simply submit to the Master.
2. Paurri 16. **Kartey key kai karnai naahi sumaar** – doings/powers of the Creator are beyond estimate.
3. Paurri 17. **Asankh Jap** – countless people focus on their duties with God in mind.
4. Paurri 18. **Asankh moorakh** - Countless people ignore God and act by self-will and commit transgressions.

---

*(**Van-u**) every plant, (**trin-u**) grass, (**tribhavan**) three regions – water, land, space – and (**paanee**) water; (**chaar-i**) four (**beyd**) Vedas and (**chaarey**) all four (**khaanee**) ways of life-creation – from egg, womb, perspiration and soil.*

*(**Khandd**) parts of the universe, (**deep**) islands and (**sabh-i**) all (**loaa** = **worlds**) continents; (**sabh-i**) all (**hoaa**) were created (**tey**) with (**eyk**) one (**kavaavai**) command of the Creator. 1.*

5. Paurri 19. **Asankh Naav**. There are countless attributes and cosmic laws of the Creator. There are Naam/laws for all; none is beyond Naam.

6. Paurri 20. **Hukmi Aavhu jaahu**, i.e. by Divine commands that souls remain in cycles of births and deaths based on the principle of as one sows so one reaps.

7. Paurri 21. **Teerath tap**. Do not argue on the time of creation; no one can know.

8. Paurri 22. **Paataala paataal.** Planets in the universe are beyond count.

9. Paurri 23. **Saalaahi Saalah-i**. The devotees praise the praiseworthy Supreme Being but do not get to know even a bit about virtues and powers of the Almighty.

10. Paurri 24. **Ant Na Siphti**. There is no limit to virtues and powers of the Almighty. Naam/Divine laws apply to the highest.

11. Paurri 25. **Bahuta Karam**. There is no limit to Divine benedictions or those seeking them. The Almighty gives but expects nothing in return.

12. Paurri 26. **Amul Gun**. Divine virtues and commands are priceless, as are those who practice them. People try to know the Creator but they cannot.

13. Paurri 27. **So dar-u.** All components of the creation function in harmony. The Almighty is the Master above all and must be obeyed.

Paurri 17

ਅਸੰਖ ਜਪ ਅਸੰਖ ਭਾਉ ॥ ਅਸੰਖ ਪੂਜਾ ਅਸੰਖ ਤਪ ਤਾਉ ॥

Asaʼnkẖ jap asaʼnkẖ bẖā▫o. Asaʼnkẖ pūjā asaʼnkẖ ṯap ṯā▫o.

*(**Asankh**) countless persons engage in (**jap**) recitation of mantras; (**asankh**) countless persons (**bhaau**) love/obey You.*

*People engage in (**asankh**) countless ways of (**pooja**) worship; and countless in (**tap**) austerities and (**taau** = **heat**) penances.*

ਅਸੰਖ ਗਰੰਥ ਮੁਖਿ ਵੇਦ ਪਾਠ ॥ ਅਸੰਖ ਜੋਗ ਮਨਿ ਰਹਹਿ ਉਦਾਸ ॥
Asaṅkẖ garanth mukẖ veḏ pāṯẖ. Asaṅkẖ jog man rahahi uḏās.

*Countless people do (**paatth**) reading of (**granth**) scriptures and (**veyd**) Vedas (**mukh-i = from mouth**) from memory.*
*Countless (**jog**) yogis (**rahah-i**) remain (**udaas**) withdrawn/unattached (**man-i**) in mind – from worldly activities.*

ਅਸੰਖ ਭਗਤ ਗੁਣ ਗਿਆਨ ਵੀਚਾਰ ॥ ਅਸੰਖ ਸਤੀ ਅਸੰਖ ਦਾਤਾਰ ॥
Asaṅkẖ bẖagaṯ guṇ gi▫ān vīcẖār. Asaṅkẖ saṯī asaṅkẖ ḏāṯār.

*Countless (**bhagat**) devotees (**veechaar**) contemplate (**giaan**) knowledge of (**gun**) Divine virtues – and cultivate them.*
*(**Asankh**) countless (**satee**) live truthfully, and countless (**daataar**) give in charity*[1].

---

[1] All the above ways are adopted with love for the Almighty. The fifth Guru says:
ਸਭਹੂ ਕੋ ਰਸੁ ਹਰਿ ਹੋ ॥੧॥ ਰਹਾਉ ॥

Sabẖhū ko ras har ho. ||1|| rahā▫o.

*(**Sabhahu**) all the following methods of worship in (**ras-u = relish**) love of (**har-i**) the Almighty. 1.*

Pause here and reflect.

ਕਾਹੂ ਜੋਗ ਕਾਹੂ ਭੋਗ ਕਾਹੂ ਗਿਆਨ ਕਾਹੂ ਧਿਆਨ ॥ ਕਾਹੂ ਹੋ ਡੰਡ ਧਰਿ ਹੋ ॥੧॥

ਅਸੰਖ ਸੂਰ ਮੁਹ ਭਖ ਸਾਰ ॥ ਅਸੰਖ ਮੋਨਿ ਲਿਵ ਲਾਇ ਤਾਰ ॥
Asaⁿkẖ sūr muh bẖakẖ sār. Asaⁿkẖ mon liv lā▫e ṯār.

*Countless (**soor**) warriors (**bhakh = eat**) receive hits of (**saar = iron**) weapons on (**muh**) face, i.e. face the enemy head on.*
*Countless (**mon-i**) silent sages (**laaey**) maintain (**taar**) continuous (**liv**) attention within, i.e. meditate.*

ਕੁਦਰਤਿ ਕਵਣ ਕਹਾ ਵੀਚਾਰੁ ॥ ਵਾਰਿਆ ਨ ਜਾਵਾ ਏਕ ਵਾਰ ॥
Kuḏraṯ kavaṇ kahā vīcẖār. vāri▫ā na jāvā ek vār.

*(**Kavan**) what (**veechaar-u**) view can I (**kahaa = say**) express on Your (**kaudrat-i**) powers; and not (**jaava = be, vaariaa = sacrifice**) submit (**eyk = one, vaar = time**) once for all, i.e. I place myself in Divine care and obedience with no questions asked, o Creator*

ਜੋ ਤੁਧੁ ਭਾਵੈ ਸਾਈ ਭਲੀ ਕਾਰ ॥ ਤੂ ਸਦਾ ਸਲਾਮਤਿ ਨਿਰੰਕਾਰ ॥੧੭॥
Jo ṯuḏẖ bẖāvai sā▫ī bẖalī kār. Ŧū saḏā salāmaṯ nirankār. ||17||

*(**Jo**) whatever (**bhaavai**) pleases (**tudh-u**) You, (**saaee**) that (**kaar**) action is (**bhalee**) good.*

Kāhū jog kāhū bẖog kāhū gi▫ān kāhū ḏẖi▫ān. Kāhū ho dand ḏẖar ho. ||1||

*(**Kaahu**) some do it through (**jog**) Yoga, for some it is by (**bhog**) making offerings of food; some do it through (**giaan**) acquiring knowledge of the scriptures and others through (**dhiaan**) meditation. Some – the yogis - wander (**ddandd dhar-i**) with staff in hand. 1.*

*And, (**too**) you are (**sadaa**) ever (**salaamat-i** = **imperishable**) present and unchanging. 17.*

Paurri 18

ਅਸੰਖ ਮੂਰਖ ਅੰਧ ਘੋਰ ॥ ਅਸੰਖ ਚੋਰ ਹਰਾਮਖੋਰ ॥ ਅਸੰਖ ਅਮਰ ਕਰਿ ਜਾਹਿ ਜੋਰ ॥

Asaʼnkẖ mūrakẖ anḏẖ gẖor. Asaʼnkẖ cẖor harāmkẖor. Asaʼnkẖ amar kar jāhi jor.

*(**Asankh**) countless persons (**moorakh** = **foolish**) act in (**ghor** = **intense**) total (**andh** = **blindness**) ignorance.*
*Countless people are (**chor**) thieves and (**haraamkhor** = **eating forbidden food**) take un-deserved advantage or misappropriate.*
*Countless people in authority/power (**kar-i jaah-i**) impose their (**amar**) authority with (**jor**) force unfairly.*

ਅਸੰਖ ਗਲਵਢ ਹਤਿਆ ਕਮਾਹਿ ॥ ਅਸੰਖ ਪਾਪੀ ਪਾਪੁ ਕਰਿ ਜਾਹਿ ॥ ਅਸੰਖ ਕੂੜਿਆਰ ਕੂੜੇ ਫਿਰਾਹਿ ॥

Asaʼnkẖ galvadẖ haṯi▫ā kamāhi. Asaʼnkẖ pāpī pāp kar jāhi. Asaʼnkẖ kūṛi▫ār kūṛe firāhi.

*Countless (**galvaddh** = **cut throats**) killers (**kamaah-i**) commit (**hatiaa**) murders.*
*Countless (**paapi**) transgressors (**kar-i jaah-i**) keep committing (**paap-u**) transgression – it becomes their nature.*
*Countless pretenders (**koorriaar**) live by falsehood/pretence and (**phiraah-i**) go about as (**koorrey** = **false**) impostors.*

ਅਸੰਖ ਮਲੇਛ ਮਲੁ ਭਖਿ ਖਾਹਿ ॥ ਅਸੰਖ ਨਿੰਦਕ ਸਿਰਿ ਕਰਹਿ ਭਾਰੁ ॥

Asa'nkh malechh mal bhakh khāhi. Asa'nkh nindak sir karahi bhār.

*Countless (**maleychh = outcasts**) people with evil minds (**bhakh-i khaah-i = eat**) consume (**mal-u**) dirt i.e. receive illegal gratification/ bribes. They take what is not theirs[1].*

*Countless (**nindak**) slanderers indulge in slander and thus (**karah-i = do**) put (**bhaar-u**) the load (**sir-i**) on their heads, i.e. face consequences of the fault of those they slander – rather than be able to harm others, they get a bad name in the world and are dealt with by Divine justice.*

ਨਾਨਕੁ ਨੀਚੁ ਕਹੈ ਵੀਚਾਰੁ ॥ ਵਾਰਿਆ ਨ ਜਾਵਾ ਏਕ ਵਾਰ ॥

Nānak nīch kahai vīchār. vāri◌ā na jāvā ek vār.

*(**Neech-u**) lowly Nanak (**kahai = says**) has expressed this (**veechaar-u**) thought and says.*

*One says such things but why don't I (**jaava = be, vaariaa = sacrifice**) submit myself (**eyk = one,***

---

[1] Guru Nanak says:

ਹਕੁ ਪਰਾਇਆ ਨਾਨਕਾ ਉਸੁ ਸੂਅਰ ਉਸੁ ਗਾਇ ॥ ਗੁਰੁ ਪੀਰੁ ਹਾਮਾ ਤਾ ਭਰੇ ਜਾ ਮੁਰਦਾਰੁ ਨ ਖਾਇ ॥

Mėhlā 1. Hak parā◌i◌ā nānkā us sū◌ar us gā◌e. Gur pīr hāmā ṯā bhare jā murdār na khā◌e.

*Slok/prologue of the first Guru: Appropriating what belongs to others is like (**sooar**) swine meat for (**us = that**) the Muslim and (**gaaey**) cow's meat for (**us = that**) the Hindu which are forbidden. The Hindu's guru and the Muslim's (**pir**) guru support (**ta**) only then (**ja**) if (**na khaaey) do not eat the meat of dead animal which is forbidden**) do not receive illegal gratification or misaapropriate. M: 1, p 141.*

***vaar* = *time*)** *once for all, i.e. I place myself in Divine care and obedience with no questions asked, o Creator*

ਜੋ ਤੁਧੁ ਭਾਵੈ ਸਾਈ ਭਲੀ ਕਾਰ ॥ ਤੂ ਸਦਾ ਸਲਾਮਤਿ ਨਿਰੰਕਾਰ ॥੧੮॥
Jo tuḏẖ bẖāvai sā▫ī bẖalī kār. Ŧū saḏā salāmaṯ nirankār. ||18||

*(**Jo**) whatever (**bhaavai**) pleases (**tudh-u**) You, (**saaee**) that is (**kaar**) action is (**bhalee**) good.*
*And, (**too**) you are (**sadaa**) ever (**salaamat-i** = **imperishable**) present and unchanging. 18.*

As may be noted, Paurri 18 uses the expression 'Nanak neech kahai veechaar' in place of 'Kudrat kavan kahaa veechaar' in Paurris 16, 17 and 19. Calling himself lowly, Guru Nanak has used this to say in humility that he has just mentioned attributes oconsidered evil and is not criticising anyone.

Paurri 19.

ਅਸੰਖ ਨਾਵ ਅਸੰਖ ਥਾਵ ॥ ਅਗੰਮ ਅਗੰਮ ਅਸੰਖ ਲੋਅ ॥ ਅਸੰਖ ਕਹਹਿ ਸਿਰਿ ਭਾਰੁ ਹੋਇ ॥
Asaʼnkẖ nāv asaʼnkẖ thāv. Agamm agamm asaʼnkẖ lo▫a. Asaʼnkẖ kėhahi sir bẖār ho▫e.

*There are (**asankh**) countless (**naav/naam**) cosmic laws*
*covering (**asankh**) the countless (**thaav**) places, i.e. cosmic laws apply everywhere.*
*There are countless (**loa/lok**) planets (**agamm**) beyond reach and (**agamm**) farther and farther where the Creator is present – and cosmic laws apply.*
*But, (**kahah-i**) calling them (**asankh**) countless (**hoey**) puts (**bhaar-u**) load (**sir-i**) on the head, i.e. one can never complete the count.*

Note: The next four lines use the term ਅਖਰੀ Akhree meaning with words/writing – as ordained. The verse after that says "jin-i ih likhey tis-u sir-i naah-i" meaning they do not apply to the One who wrote them. Therefore, these 'Akhar' are Divine commands/cosmic laws which were created before the universe came into being.

ਅਖਰੀ ਨਾਮੁ ਅਖਰੀ ਸਾਲਾਹ ॥ ਅਖਰੀ ਗਿਆਨੁ ਗੀਤ ਗੁਣ ਗਾਹ ॥ ਅਖਰੀ ਲਿਖਣੁ ਬੋਲਣੁ ਬਾਣਿ ॥ ਅਖਰਾ ਸਿਰਿ ਸੰਜੋਗੁ ਵਖਾਣਿ ॥

Akẖrī nām akẖrī sālāh. Akẖrī gi▫ān gīt̲ guṇ gāh. Akẖrī likẖaṇ bolaṇ bāṇ. Akẖrā sir sanjog vakẖāṇ.

*The creatures act as the Creator directs; they obey (**naam-u**) Naam/Divine commands (**akhree = by words/writing**) with Divine directions, i.e. when motivated from within; they (**saalaah**) praise and emulate Divine virtues when motivated from within.*
*It is with (**akhree**) Divine directions/motivation that they obtain (**giaan**) awareness and (**gaah**) sing (**geet**) songs praising (**gun**) Divine virtues.*
*(**Likhan-u**) writing, (**bolan-u**) speaking and (**baan-i/bantar = making**) imbibing is (**akhri**) by Divine motivation.*
*(**Sanjog-u**) union with the Almighty is attained by (**vakhaan-i = saying**) praising and obeying (**akhraa**) commands (**sir-i = on the head**) as applicable for everyone.*

ਜਿਨਿ ਏਹਿ ਲਿਖੇ ਤਿਸੁ ਸਿਰਿ ਨਾਹਿ ॥ ਜਿਵ ਫੁਰਮਾਏ ਤਿਵ ਤਿਵ ਪਾਹਿ ॥

Jin ehi likẖe t̲is sir nāhi. Jiv furmā▫e t̲iv t̲iv pāhi.

*However, these laws are not applicable to (**tis-u = that**) the Creator (**jin-i**) who (**likhey**) wrote them; (**jiv**) as the Creator (**phurmaaey**) ordains the creatures (**paah-i**) receive (**tiv tiv**) likewise, i.e.get their roles with applicable directions.*

ਜੇਤਾ ਕੀਤਾ ਤੇਤਾ ਨਾਉ ॥ ਵਿਣੁ ਨਾਵੈ ਨਾਹੀ ਕੋ ਥਾਉ ॥
Jeṯā kīṯā ṯeṯā nā▫o. viṇ nāvai nāhī ko thā▫o.

*(**Jeyta**) as are the numbers of (**keetaa**) those created, (**teyta**) that many are (**naau**) commands/cosmic laws, i.e. every-one/thing is subject to Divine laws applicable to them.*
*There is (**naahee ko = not any**) no (**thaau**) place (**vin-u**) without (**naavai**) Naam/Divine law applicable.*

But, what are all those places, what all comprises the universe? There is no complete answer possible for this since the expanse of creation is beyond human comprehension. We must acknowledge this and say:

ਕੁਦਰਤਿ ਕਵਣ ਕਹਾ ਵੀਚਾਰੁ ॥ ਵਾਰਿਆ ਨ ਜਾਵਾ ਏਕ ਵਾਰ ॥
Kuḏraṯ kavaṇ kahā vīcẖār. vāri▫ā na jāvā ek vār.

*(**Kavan**) what (**veechaar-u**) view can I (**kahaa = say**) express on Your (**kaudrat-i**) powers; and not (**jaava = be, vaariaa = sacrifice**) submit (**eyk = one, vaar = time**) once for all, i.e. I place myself in Divine care and obedience with no questions asked, o Creator*

ਜੋ ਤੁਧੁ ਭਾਵੈ ਸਾਈ ਭਲੀ ਕਾਰ ॥ ਤੂ ਸਦਾ ਸਲਾਮਤਿ ਨਿਰੰਕਾਰ ॥੧੯॥
Jo ṯuḏẖ bẖāvai sā▫ī bẖalī kār. Ŧū saḏā salāmaṯ nirankār. ||19||

*(**Jo**) whatever (**bhaavai**) pleases (**tudh-u**) You, (**saaee**) that is (**kaar**) action is (**bhalee**) good.*
*(**Too**) you are (**sadaa**) ever (**salaamat-i = imperishable**) present and unchanging. 19.*

Paurri 20.

ਭਰੀਐ ਹਥੁ ਪੈਰੁ ਤਨੁ ਦੇਹ ॥ ਪਾਣੀ ਧੋਤੈ ਉਤਰਸੁ ਖੇਹ ॥ ਮੂਤ ਪਲੀਤੀ ਕਪੜੁ ਹੋਇ ॥ ਦੇ ਸਾਬੂਣੁ ਲਈਐ ਓਹੁ ਧੋਇ ॥

Bẖarī▫ai hath pair ṯan ḏeh. Pāṇī ḏẖoṯai uṯras kẖeh. Mūṯ palīṯī kapaṛ ho▫e. Ḏe sābūṇ la▫ī▫ai oh ḏẖo▫e.

*(**Tan-u**) the subtle body/mind and (**deyh**) the body like (**hath-u**) hand and (**pair-u**) foot (**bhareeai**) become dirty and (**dhotai**) washing with (**paanee**) water (**utras-u**) removes (**kheyh**) the dirt.*
*When (**kaparr-u**) a garment (**hoey**) is soiled with (**moot**) urine or (**paleetee**) with faeces; it is (**laeeai dhoey**) washed (**dey**) with water and (**saaboon-u**) soap.*

ਭਰੀਐ ਮਤਿ ਪਾਪਾ ਕੈ ਸੰਗਿ ॥ ਓਹੁ ਧੋਪੈ ਨਾਵੈ ਕੈ ਰੰਗਿ ॥

Bẖarī▫ai maṯ pāpā kai sang. Oh ḏẖopai nāvai kai rang.

*Similarly, (**mat-i**) the mind keeps getting (**bhareeai**) defiled (**kai = of, sang-i = company**) with (**paapa = sins**) carnal thoughts and actions. (**Oh-u**) that (**dhopai = washed**) is cleansed (**rang-i = with love**) with remembrance and obedience (**naavai**) to the Almighty.*

Note: The above is achieved by focussing on Nitnem, the daily-prescribed reading for the Sikh. The Baanis/compositions prescribed to be read and contemplated contain the instructions to follow. The content of Nitnem has been selected by the fifth Guru and given on pages 1-13, and 1429 of Sri Guru Granth Sahib. Baanis of the tenth Guru have been added later as part of Sikh Rahat Maryada, the Sikh code of conduct.

ਪੁੰਨੀ ਪਾਪੀ ਆਖਣੁ ਨਾਹਿ ॥ ਕਰਿ ਕਰਿ ਕਰਣਾ ਲਿਖਿ ਲੈ ਜਾਹੁ ॥ਆਪੇ ਬੀਜਿ ਆਪੇ ਹੀ ਖਾਹੁ ॥ ਨਾਨਕ ਹੁਕਮੀ ਆਵਹੁ ਜਾਹੁ ॥੨੦॥

Punnī pāpī ākẖaṇ nāhi. Kar kar karṇā likẖ lai jāhu. Āpe bīj āpe hī kẖāhu. Nānak hukmī āvhu jāhu. ||20||

*One does not become (**punnee**) virtuous or (**paapee**) a transgressor (**aakhan-u = saying**) by words. It is by (**kar-i kar-i karnaa = acting – thrice**) by thoughts, words and deeds; all these (**likh-i**) written on the mind/soul to affect future conduct, and (**lai jaah-u**) taken to the hereafter by the soul – where it has to account for them to Divine justice and face consequences.*

Positive or negative *consequences are experienced based on the principle that what (**aapey = self**) one (**beejai**) sows, (**hi**) only s/he (**aapey**) him/her-self (**khaah-u = eats**) gets/faces the consequences.*

*One who transgresses, keeps (**aavh-u = comes**) being born and (**jaah-u = goes**) dying, (**hukmi = by orders**) as is the Divine law, says Guru Nanak. 20.*

Preface to Paurris 21-23

These Paurris emphasise that rituals are of no help in cleansing the self. Paurri 6 had talked of rituals like ceremonial baths at pilgrimage centres and said that the test is whether God is pleased. Actions of "Suniaa mania man-i keeta bhaau" listening, accepting, obeying and loving keeping in mind, in Paurri 5. Paurri 21 reiterates this. Paurris 21 and 22 also ask to refrain from arguments on subjects beyond human awareness. Paurri 21 on the time of creation and 22 on its composition. Paurri 23 emphasises humility.

ਤੀਰਥੁ ਤਪੁ ਦਇਆ ਦਤੁ ਦਾਨੁ ॥ ਜੇ ਕੋ ਪਾਵੈ ਤਿਲ ਕਾ ਮਾਨੁ ॥

Ŧirath ṯap ḏa▫i▫ā ḏaṯ ḏān. Je ko pāvai ṯil kā mān.

*(**Teerath-u**) pilgrimage, (**tap-u**) austerity/self-denial, (**daiaa**) compassion (**dat-u = given**) giving (**daan-u**) charity; (**jey**) if (**ko**) someone does these, s/he (**paavai**) receives (**ka = of, til = sesame seed/small**) short term (**maan-u**) recognition/fame.*

ਸੁਣਿਆ ਮੰਨਿਆ ਮਨਿ ਕੀਤਾ ਭਾਉ ॥ ਅੰਤਰਗਤਿ ਤੀਰਥਿ ਮਲਿ ਨਾਉ ॥
Suṇi▫ā mani▫ā man kīṯā bẖā▫o. Anṯargaṯ ṯirath mal nā▫o.

*One who (**ma'nniaa**) listens, (**ma'nniaa**) obeys and (**keetaa bhaau = does with love**) lovingly keeps Naam (**man-i**) in mind, (**naau = bathes**) washes off (**mal-i**) the dirt of evil from within (**teerath-i**) at the pilgrimage of (**antargat-i = antar = inside + gat-i = freedom**) inner purification – this is how mind is cleared of other ideas and God/peace experienced within.*

ਸਭਿ ਗੁਣ ਤੇਰੇ ਮੈ ਨਾਹੀ ਕੋਇ ॥ ਵਿਣੁ ਗੁਣ ਕੀਤੇ ਭਗਤਿ ਨ ਹੋਇ ॥
Sabẖ guṇ ṯere mai nāhī ko▫e. viṇ guṇ kīṯe bẖagaṯ na ho▫e.

*O Almighty, (**sabh-i**) all (**gun-i**) virtues/capabilities are (**teyrey**) Yours; (**mai**) I have (**naahi koey = not any**) none, and know none of Yours.*
*(**Bhagat-i**) devotion/obedience does not (**hoey**) come without You (**keetey**) making me aware of Your (**gun**) virtues and commands – therefore please impart awareness of virtues and commands to me.*

Note: The message from the above is that base ideas mask the mind and one cannot recognise the Divine within. When the Almighty is kind to lead to the guru who helps dispel carnal thoughts, one gets the Divine experience. This translates to being at peace with the Self, in a state of poise.

ਸੁਅਸਤਿ ਆਥਿ ਬਾਣੀ ਬਰਮਾਉ ॥ ਸਤਿ ਸੁਹਾਣੁ ਸਦਾ ਮਨਿ ਚਾਉ ॥
Su▫asaṯ āth baṇī barmā▫o. Saṯ suhāṇ saḏā man cẖā▫o.

*I (**suast-i = glory be to**) adore You for granting (**aath-i = economic well-being**) the wherewithal and (**barmaau**) comforting (**baanee= words**) Divine messages within.*
*I (**sadaa**) forever have (**chaau**) yearning (**man-i**) in mind to have vision of Your (**sat-i**) eternal (**suhaan-u**) beauty within and in Your creation.*

This Paurri further asks people to just obey the Creator and
not get into arguments about when the creation came into being, for none except the Creator knows it, thus:

ਕਵਣੁ ਸੁ ਵੇਲਾ ਵਖਤੁ ਕਵਣੁ ਕਵਣ ਥਿਤਿ ਕਵਣੁ ਵਾਰੁ ॥ ਕਵਣਿ ਸਿ ਰੁਤੀ ਮਾਹੁ ਕਵਣੁ ਜਿਤੁ ਹੋਆ ਆਕਾਰੁ ॥
Kavaṇ suvelā vakẖaṯ kavaṇ kavaṇ thiṯ kavaṇ vār. Kava ṇ sė ruṯī māhu kavaṇ jiṯ ho▫ā ākār.

Question: *(**Kavan-u**) what was (**su**) that (**veyla = Hindu expression for time, vakhat-u = Muslim expression for time**) time of the day, what (**thit-i**) day in the lunar cycle, and what (**vaar-u**) day of the week;*
*(**kavan-i**) in which (**ruti**) season, and (**maah-u**) month of the year (**s-i**) it was (**jit-u**) when (**aakaar-u**) the physical creation (**hoaa = happened**) came into being?*

And, answers:

ਵੇਲ ਨ ਪਾਈਆ ਪੰਡਤੀ ਜਿ ਹੋਵੈ ਲੇਖੁ ਪੁਰਾਣੁ ॥ ਵਖਤੁ ਨ ਪਾਇਓ ਕਾਦੀਆ ਜਿ ਲਿਖਨਿ ਲੇਖੁ ਕੁਰਾਣੁ ॥

vel na pā▫ī▫ā pandṯī jė hovai lekẖ purāṇ. vakẖaṯ na pā▫i▫o kāḏī▫ā jė likẖan lekẖ kurāṇ.

*(**Panddtee**) the Hindu scholars did not (**paaeeaa**) find/know (**veyl/veyla**) the time, (**j-i**) that they could have (**keykh-u**) written in (**puraan-u**) a Purana. (**Kadeeaa/Kaazis**) the Muslim scholars did not (**paaio**) find/know (**vakht-u**) the time (**j-i**) that they could have (**likhan-i**) written (**leykh-u = writing**) this in (**kuraan-u**) the Quran.*

ਥਿਤਿ ਵਾਰੁ ਨਾ ਜੋਗੀ ਜਾਣੈ ਰੁਤਿ ਮਾਹੁ ਨਾ ਕੋਈ ॥ ਜਾ ਕਰਤਾ ਸਿਰਠੀ ਕਉ ਸਾਜੇ ਆਪੇ ਜਾਣੈ ਸੋਈ ॥

Thiṯ vār nā jogī jāṇai ruṯ māhu nā ko▫ī. Jā karṯā sirṯẖī ka▫o sāje āpe jāṇai so▫ī.

*The Yogi (**na jaanai**) does not know (**thit-i**) the day of the*
*lunar cycle or (**vaar-u**) day of the week; (**na koee**) no one knows (**rut-i**) the season or (**maah-u**) the month. (**Karta**) the Creator (**soee = that one**) alone (**jaanai**) knows (**ja**) when IT (**saajey**) made (**sirtthi/srishtti**) the universe.*

The Paurri continues:

ਕਿਵ ਕਰਿ ਆਖਾ ਕਿਵ ਸਾਲਾਹੀ ਕਿਉ ਵਰਨੀ ਕਿਵ ਜਾਣਾ ॥ ਨਾਨਕ ਆਖਣਿ ਸਭੁ ਕੋ ਆਖੈ ਇਕ ਦੂ ਇਕੁ ਸਿਆਣਾ ॥

Kiv kar ākẖā kiv sālāhī ki▫o varnī kiv jāṇā. Nānak ākẖaṇ sabẖ ko ākẖai ik ḏū ik si▫āṇā.

*(**Kiv kar-i = how**) with what should I (**aakhaa**) describe, (**kiv**) which way do I (**saalaahee**) praise the*

*Creator, or (**varnee**) mention, and (**kiv**) how do I (**jaanaa**) know the origin of creation?*
*(**Sabh-u ko**) everyone (**aakhai**) says something (**aakhaan-i**) for the sake of saying, with (**ik-u**) one trying to be (**siaanaa**) wiser (**doo**) than (**ik**) another, i.e. they outdo one another in display of wisdom.*

But it is futile:

ਵਡਾ ਸਾਹਿਬੁ ਵਡੀ ਨਾਈ ਕੀਤਾ ਜਾ ਕਾ ਹੋਵੈ ॥ ਨਾਨਕ ਜੇ ਕੋ ਆਪੌ ਜਾਣੈ ਅਗੈ ਗਇਆ ਨ ਸੋਹੈ ॥੨੧॥
vadā sāhib vadī nā▫ī kīṯā jā kā hovai. Nānak je ko āpou jāṇai agai ga▫i▫ā na sohai. ||21||

*(**Sahib-u**) the Master is (**vaddaa**) great having (**vaddee**) supreme (**naaee**) Naam/authority, (**ja kaa**) whose (**keetaa**) creation everything (**hovai = happens**) is, i.e. the Creator alone knows.*
*(**Jey**) if (**ko**) someone (**jaanai**) considers (**aapou**) the self – all-knowing as the Creator does, s/he does not (**sohai = look good**) receive honour (**agai gaiaa = going forward**) later as s/he cannot prove, says Guru Nanak. 21.*

Paurri 22

The Guru now refers to the arguments regarding composition of the universe in Eastern and Semitic scriptures.

ਪਾਤਾਲਾ ਪਾਤਾਲ ਲਖ ਆਗਾਸਾ ਆਗਾਸ ॥ ਓੜਕ ਓੜਕ ਭਾਲਿ ਥਕੇ ਵੇਦ ਕਹਨਿ ਇਕ ਵਾਤ ॥
Pāṯālā pāṯāl lakẖ āgāsā āgās. Oṛak oṛak bẖāl thake veḏ kahan ik vāṯ.

*There are lakhs of (**paataala paataal**) regions below the earth and lakhs of (**aagaasa agaas**) skies, i.e.*

there are lakhs of planets with their skies and the lower regions.
*Those (**bhaal-i**) searching for (**orrak**) end/boundary of creation (**orrak**) ultimately (**thakey**) get tired, i.e. give up, (**veyd**) the Vedas (**kahan-i**) say this with (**ik**) one (**vaat**) voice - that efforts to find them do not succeed.*

ਸਹਸ ਅਠਾਰਹ ਕਹਨਿ ਕਤੇਬਾ ਅਸੁਲੂ ਇਕੁ ਧਾਤੁ ॥
Sahas aṯẖārah kahan kaṯebā asulū ik ḏẖāṯ.

(***Kateyba***) *the Semitic scriptures (**kahan-i**) say there are (**atthaarah**) eighteen (**sahas**) thousand planets but their (**asloo**) source is (**ik-u**) the One (**dhaat-u**) Creator.*

ਲੇਖਾ ਹੋਇ ਤ ਲਿਖੀਐ ਲੇਖੈ ਹੋਇ ਵਿਣਾਸੁ ॥ ਨਾਨਕ ਵਡਾ ਆਖੀਐ ਆਪੇ ਜਾਣੈ ਆਪੁ ॥੨੨॥
Lekẖā ho▫e ṯa likī▫ai lekẖai ho▫e viṇās. Nānak vadā ākẖī▫ai āpe jāṇai āp. ||22||

*We can (**likheeay**) write the count only if (**leykha**) count (**hoey**) is possible; anyone (**leykhai**) counting (**hoey = happens, vinaas-u = destruction**) dies, but the count is not complete.*
*We should (**aakheeai = say**) acknowledge that (**vaddaa**) the great Creator (**aapai**) IT-self created and (**aap-u**) IT-self alone (**jaanai**) knows, - about the whole creation and no creature can know, says Guru Nanak. 22.*

Note: Reference to 18000 planets does not exist in any of the main Semitic scriptures i.e. the Hebrew Bible/Old Testament, the Christian New Testament, or the Muslim Quran. It however exists in the Talmud, a record of oral discussions pertaining to the Jewish Law between the Rabbis, the Jewish clergy, and considered authoritative. It says God flies through 18000 worlds or planets (Talmud - Aveda Zara 3b). Guru Nanak's knowledge of this shows he had interacted with the Jews, although there is no historical record available.

Paurri 23

ਸਾਲਾਹੀ ਸਾਲਾਹਿ ਏਤੀ ਸੁਰਤਿ ਨ ਪਾਈਆ ॥ ਨਦੀਆ ਅਤੈ ਵਾਹ ਪਵਹਿ ਸਮੁੰਦਿ ਨ ਜਾਣੀਅਹਿ ॥

Sālāhī sālāhi eṯī suraṯ na pā▫ī▫ā. Naḏī▫ā aṯai vāh pavahi samunḏ na jāṇī▫ahi.

*The devotees (**salaah-i**) praise/obey (**saalaah-i**) the praiseworthy Almighty but (**na paaeeaa**) get (**eyti = this much**) little (**surat-i**) awareness about the Master.*
*They remain absorbed in the Almighty, like (**nadeeaa**) the rivers and (**vaahu**) streams which keep moving to the sea and (**na jaaneeah-i = are not known**) lose their identity when they (**pavah-i**) enter (**samund-i**) the sea.*

Note: There is another aspect. Most rivers start from hills encountering rocks on the way and seem turbulent; but when they enter the planes, they become calm and steady. Similarly, one seeking the Almighty initially faces obstacles in the form of temptations and wavering. Perseverance leads to peace and being absorbed in God, like the rivers lose their identity on entering the sea.

The grace so obtained is more powerful than anything of material nature, says the next line:

ਸਮੁੰਦ ਸਾਹ ਸੁਲਤਾਨ ਗਿਰਹਾ ਸੇਤੀ ਮਾਲੁ ਧਨੁ ॥ ਕੀੜੀ ਤੁਲਿ ਨ ਹੋਵਨੀ ਜੇ ਤਿਸੁ ਮਨਹੁ ਨ ਵੀਸਰਹਿ ॥੨੩॥

Samund sāh sultān girhā setī māl dhan. Kīrī tul na hovnī je tis manhu na vīsrahi. ||23||

*(**Saah**) kings and (**sultaan**) emperors (**seyti = with**) having dominion as big as (**samund**) the ocean, with mountains of (**maal-u**) possessions and (**dhan-u**) wealth; these persons of high status (**hovnee = be**)* are *not (**tul-i**) equal – in receiving Divine evaluation – to the little (**keerree**) ant (**jey = if, tis-u = that**) by whose (**manhu**) mind the Almighty is not (**veesarah-i**) forgotten. 23.*

In other words, perseverance in obedience, like the river waters flowing to the sea despite obstacles is the key to finding the Almighty.

<u>Paurri 24</u>

Paurris 24 to 27 show magnificence of the Supreme Being from different angles. Paurri says 24 the Creator, the Creator's creation and authority are infinite. Naam/Divine commands/natural laws apply to the highest.

ਅੰਤੁ ਨ ਸਿਫਤੀ ਕਹਣਿ ਨ ਅੰਤੁ ॥ ਅੰਤੁ ਨ ਕਰਣੈ ਦੇਣਿ ਨ ਅੰਤੁ ॥
Ant na siftī kahaṇ na ant. Ant na karṇai deṇ na ant.

*There is no (**ant-u**) end (**siphtee**) to attributes, i.e. virtues and powers, of the Almighty; nor (**ant-u**) end to count of those who (**kahan-i = say**) praise.*
*There is no (**ant-u**) end to (**karnai = doings**) the creation and to (**deyn-i = giving**) provisions made in it for the creatures.*

ਅੰਤੁ ਨ ਵੇਖਣਿ ਸੁਣਣਿ ਨ ਅੰਤੁ ॥ ਅੰਤੁ ਨ ਜਾਪੈ ਕਿਆ ਮਨਿ ਮੰਤੁ ॥
Ant na vekhaṇ suṇaṇ na ant. Ant na jāpai ki▫ā man mant.

*There is no (**ant-u**) end (**veykhan-i**) to seeing the expanse of creation; and, (**sunan-i**) hearing description of creation never (**ant-u**) ends.*
*(**Ant-u**) extent of (**kiaa**) what (**mant-u/mantav**) intention the Creator has (**man-i**) in mind cannot (**jaapai**) be perceived, i.e. no one knows what is going to happen in future.*

ਅੰਤੁ ਨ ਜਾਪੈ ਕੀਤਾ ਆਕਾਰੁ ॥ ਅੰਤੁ ਨ ਜਾਪੈ ਪਾਰਾਵਾਰੁ ॥
Anṯ na jāpai kīṯā ākār. Anṯ na jāpai pārāvār.

*(**Ant-u**) extent of (**keeta = made, aakaar-u = form**) the creation cannot (**jaapai**) be perceived/known.*
*There is no (**paaraavaar-u**) near end or far (**ant-u**) end – the creation is infinite.*

ਅੰਤ ਕਾਰਣਿ ਕੇਤੇ ਬਿਲਲਾਹਿ ॥ ਤਾ ਕੇ ਅੰਤ ਨ ਪਾਏ ਜਾਹਿ ॥
Anṯ kāraṇ keṯe billāhi. Ŧā ke anṯ na pā▫e jāhi.

*(**Keytey = how many**) countless seekers (**bil-laah-i = agonise**) strongly yearn/try hard (**kaaran-i**) for the sake of knowing (**ant**) extent of creation/the Creator's domain; (**ta = they, key = of**) their (**ant-u = limit**) count (**na jaah-i**) cannot be (**paah-i = obtained**) known.*

ਏਹੁ ਅੰਤੁ ਨ ਜਾਣੈ ਕੋਇ ॥ ਬਹੁਤਾ ਕਹੀਐ ਬਹੁਤਾ ਹੋਇ ॥-
Ėhu anṯ na jāṇai ko▫e. Bahuṯā kahī▫ai bahuṯā ho▫e.

*(**Na koey**) no one (**jaanai**) knows (**ant-u**) the end of all (**ih**) this, i.e. of the Creator and the seekers. (**Bahuta**) the more (**kaheeai**) we say, there (**hoey**) is still (**bahuta**) more left to be said – with no end.*

ਵਡਾ ਸਾਹਿਬੁ ਊਚਾ ਥਾਉ ॥ ਊਚੇ ਉਪਰਿ ਊਚਾ ਨਾਉ ॥

vadā sāhib ūcẖā thā▫o. Ūcẖe upar ūcẖā nā▫o.

*(**Sahib-u**) the Master is (**vaddaa**) great and has (**oochaa**) high (**thaau = place**) authority.*

*God's (**naau**) Naam/writ/authority applies (**upar-i**) over (**oochey**) the highest.*

ਏਵਡੁ ਊਚਾ ਹੋਵੈ ਕੋਇ ॥ ਤਿਸੁ ਊਚੇ ਕਉ ਜਾਣੈ ਸੋਇ ॥ ਜੇਵਡੁ ਆਪਿ ਜਾਣੈ ਆਪਿ ਆਪਿ ॥ ਨਾਨਕ ਨਦਰੀ ਕਰਮੀ ਦਾਤਿ ॥੨੪॥

Ėvad ūcẖā hovai ko▫e. Ŧis ūcẖe ka▫o jāṇai so▫e. Jevad āp jāṇai āp āp. Nānak naḏrī karmī ḏāṯ. ||24||

*Only (**koey**) someone who (**hovai**) is (**eyvadd-u**) as great and (**oocha**) high, (**soey**) that (**jaanai**) knows (**oochey kau**) the high/great (**tis-u = that**) Almighty Master – but there is none.*

*(**Jeyvadd**) how great (**aap-i = self**) the Almighty is; that only (**aap-i**) the Almighty is, and only (**aap-i**) IT-self (**jaanai**) knows.*

*The great Almighty gives great (**daat-i**) benedictions and bestows (**nadree = sight of grace**) grace (**karmi**) based on deeds, says Guru Nanak. 24.*

Paurri 25

ਬਹੁਤਾ ਕਰਮੁ ਲਿਖਿਆ ਨਾ ਜਾਇ ॥ ਵਡਾ ਦਾਤਾ ਤਿਲੁ ਨ ਤਮਾਇ ॥

Bahuṯā karam likẖi▫ā nā jā▫e. vadā ḏāṯā ṯil na ṯamā▫e.

*(**Karam-u = grace**) benedictions of the Almighty are (**bahutaa**) plentiful, they (**na jaaey**) cannot (**likhiaa**) be written on paper, i.e. no length of paper is enough. The Supreme Being is (**vaddaa = great**) highly (**daataa = giver**) beneficent; has not (**til-u =***

***sesame seed)** even a bit of (**tamaaey** = **need/greed**) expectation – for giving*[1].

Note: There is a lesson in this for those who try to make deals with God through ਸੁਖਨਾ ਸੁਖਨੀ (Sukhna Sukhnee), whereby they promise offerings to God if their wishes are fulfilled. The Guru says the Almighty is above such things. So, we should not expect our prayers to be heard simply because we are offering something. As will be seen below, the Master knows who needs/deserves what, and gives; but some rare persons say this.

ਕੇਤੇ ਮੰਗਹਿ ਜੋਧ ਅਪਾਰ ॥ ਕੇਤਿਆ ਗਣਤ ਨਹੀ ਵੀਚਾਰੁ ॥

Keṯe mangahi joḏẖ apār. Keṯi▫ā gaṇaṯ nahī vīcẖār.

*(**Ketey** = **so many**) there is no dearth of (**jodh**) warriors who (**mangah-i**) ask, they are (**apaar**) infinite in number; they (**mangah-i**) beg for strength and victory in battle. One cannot (**veechaar-u**) think of (**ganat**) count of (**keytiaa**) all those who ask.*

---

[1] The fifth Guru says:
ਪਹਿਲੋ ਦੇ ਤੈਂ ਰਿਜਕੁ ਸਮਾਹਾ ॥ ਪਿਛੋ ਦੇ ਤੈ ਜੰਤੁ ਉਪਾਹਾ ॥ ਤੁਧੁ ਜੇਵਡੁ ਦਾਤਾ ਅਵਰੁ ਨ ਸੁਆਮੀ ਲਵੈ ਨ ਕੋਈ ਲਾਵਣਿਆ ॥੬॥

Pahilo ḏe ṯaiʼn rijak samāhā. Picẖẖo ḏe ṯaiʼn janṯ upāhā. Ŧuḏẖ jevad ḏāṯā avar na su▫āmī lavai na ko▫ī lāvaṇi▫ā. ||6||

*O Creator, (**tai**) You (**pahlo dey**) first (**samaahaa**) provide the (**rijak-u**) wherewithal, and (**pichho dey**) after that (**upaahaa**) create the (**jant-u**) creature; there is (**avar-u na**) no other (**daata**) benefactor (**jeyvadd-u**) as great as (**tudh-u**) You, o (**suaami**) Master; (**na koee**) no one (**laavniaa**) comes (**lavai**) near You. 6.*

ਕੇਤੇ ਖਪਿ ਤੁਟਹਿ ਵੇਕਾਰ ॥ ਕੇਤੇ ਲੈ ਲੈ ਮੁਕਰੁ ਪਾਹਿ ॥ ਕੇਤੇ ਮੂਰਖ ਖਾਹੀ ਖਾਹਿ ॥
Keṯe kẖap ṯutahi vekār. Keṯe lai lai mukar pāhi. Keṯe mūrakẖ kẖāhī kẖāhi.

*(**Keytey**) numerous persons use the benedictions but forget commands of the Creator, (**tuttah-i = break**) succumb to (**veykaar**) vices and (**khap-i**) ruin themselves.*
*(**Ketey**) numerous persons (**lai lai = keep taking**) use benedictions but (**mukar-u paah-i**) deny the Giver, i.e. claim to have achieved by their own strength.*
*(**Ketey**) numerous (**moorakh = fools**) ignorant persons (**khaahee khaah-i = keep eating**) just keep using the benedictions – but do not acknowledge the Giver.*

There are however people who are satisfied with what they have. Such people do not complain even in case of suffering
but take it as reminder of having forgotten their duties:

ਕੇਤਿਆ ਦੂਖ ਭੂਖ ਸਦ ਮਾਰ ॥ ਏਹਿ ਭਿ ਦਾਤਿ ਤੇਰੀ ਦਾਤਾਰ ॥
Keṯi▫ā ḏūkẖ bẖūkẖ saḏ mār. Ėhi bẖė ḏāṯ ṯerī ḏāṯār.

*(**Keytiaa**) many persons, (**sad**) ever being in (**dookh**) distress, (**bhookh**) hunger and (**maar = beating**) pain – do not complain but say: (**Eh-i**) this is (**bh-i**) also (**teyri**) Your (**daat-i**) benediction, o (**daataar = giver**) benevolent Master, i.e. it is a reminder for having forgotten Naam of the Almighty.*

ਬੰਦਿ ਖਲਾਸੀ ਭਾਣੈ ਹੋਇ ॥ ਹੋਰੁ ਆਖਿ ਨ ਸਕੈ ਕੋਇ ॥
Banḏ kẖalāsī bẖāṇai ho▫e. Hor ākẖ na sakai ko▫e.

*(**Band-i**) bondage to, and (**khalaasi**) freedom - from being born and experiencing comforts and discomforts – (**hoey**) happens (**bhaanai**) by Divine will, and (**na koey = not any**) no one (**hor-u**) else (**sakai**) can (**aakh-i**) say - that there is any other way.*

ਜੇ ਕੋ ਖਾਇਕੁ ਆਖਣਿ ਪਾਇ ॥ ਓਹੁ ਜਾਣੈ ਜੇਤੀਆ ਮੁਹਿ ਖਾਇ ॥
Je ko kẖā▫ik ākẖaṇ pā▫e. Oh jāṇai jeṯī▫ā muhi kẖā▫e.

*(**Jey**) if (**ko**) some (**khaaik-u = gossiper**) bragger (**aakhan-i paaey = says**) claims that ability; (**oh-u**) that person (**jaanai**) know (**jeyteeaa**) how many hits s/he (**khaaey**) receives (**muh-i**) on the face, i.e. how much s/he is disliked by others and how long s/he keeps getting rejected for union with the Almighty and is sent for rebirth.*

The Creator who created the universe provided for everything needed but some rare person acknowledges and lives in obedience of the Creator:

ਆਪੇ ਜਾਣੈ ਆਪੇ ਦੇਇ ॥ ਆਖਹਿ ਸਿ ਭਿ ਕੇਈ ਕੇਇ ॥
Āpe jāṇai āpe ḏe▫e. Ākẖahi sė bẖė ke▫ī ke▫e.

*(**Aapey = self**) the Almighty (**jaanai**) knows what everyone needs, and (**aapey**) IT-self (**dey-i**) gives – what is deserved.*
*However, (**s-i**) those who (**aakhah-i = say**) believe in this are (**bh-i**) also (**kayee key-i**) rarest of the rare.*

ਜਿਸ ਨੋ ਬਖਸੇ ਸਿਫਤਿ ਸਾਲਾਹ ॥ ਨਾਨਕ ਪਾਤਿਸਾਹੀ ਪਾਤਿਸਾਹੁ ॥੨੫॥
Jis no bakẖse sifaṯ sālāh. Nānak pāṯisāhī pāṯisāhu. ||25||

*Those (**no**) to (**jis**) whom the Almighty (**bakhsey**) bestows grace to (**saalaah**) praise and obey Divine* *commands, (**siphat-i**) Divine virtues and commands; that person is (**paatsaah-u**) the emperor (**paasaahi**) over the emperors, i.e. s/he receives honour I life and in the hereafter, says Guru Nanak.* 25.

Paurri 26 Part 1

Paurri 26 has two parts. The first part describes journey of the soul who remains conscious of Naam from birth through life, receives Divine grace, and ultimately merges with the Creator. This has been done using the allegory of business. In business, the owner of the business sends out merchants with the merchandise and expects them to bring back profit. Those who bring back profit receive recognition. In the spiritual realm, the Creator is the owner of the business/play of the creation, the creatures are the merchants, and awareness of Naam/Divine virtues and commands is the merchandise[1]. Dealing in this merchandise means conducting the self by Naam.

Everything/everyone in the above context has been called ਅਮੁਲ 'Amul', meaning 'priceless'.

ਅਮੁਲ ਗੁਣ ਅਮੁਲ ਵਾਪਾਰ ॥ ਅਮੁਲ ਵਾਪਾਰੀਏ ਅਮੁਲ ਭੰਡਾਰ ॥

Amul guṇ amul vāpār. Amul vāpārī▫e amul bẖandār.

*(**Gun**) Divine virtues and commands are (**amul**) priceless/sublime wealth and (**vaapaar**) business*

---

[1] ਮੈ ਬਨਜਾਰਨਿ ਰਾਮ ਕੀ ॥ ਤੇਰਾ ਨਾਮੁ ਵਖਰੁ ਵਾਪਾਰੁ ਜੀ ॥੧॥ ਰਹਾਉ ॥ ੧ ੧੫੭

Mai banjāran rām kī. Ŧerā nām vakẖar vāpār jī. ||1|| rahā▫o.

I am the Divine merchant; Divine virtues are the merchandise I trade in. Pause. (M: 1, p 157).

*done with these, i.e. conducting the self by Divine virtues and commands, is (**amul**) priceless.*
*(**Amul**) priceless are (**vaapaareeay**) the traders as is (**bhanddaar**) the merchandise, i.e. Naam, and those who conduct themselves by Naam, are exalted.*

ਅਮੁਲ ਆਵਹਿ ਅਮੁਲ ਲੈ ਜਾਹਿ ॥ ਅਮੁਲ ਭਾਇ ਅਮੁਲਾ ਸਮਾਹਿ ॥
Amul āvahi amul lai jāhi. Amul bẖā▫e amulā samāhi.

*Awareness of (**amul**) the priceless/valuable virtues and commands (**aavah-i**) comes with the soul, and if they conduct themselves accordingly, they (**jaah-i**) depart (**lai**) taking taking compliance with (**amul**) priceless Divine commands, with them as credit.*
*Such persons (**bhaaey = liked**) are approved by (**amul**) the Almighty and (**samaah-i**) merge (**amulaa**) in the priceless/Supreme Being*[1]*.*
Every soul is evaluated for compliance with Naam/commands. The metaphoric judge in Divine

---

[1] Guru Nanak says elsewhere:
ਵਾਪਾਰੀ ਵਣਜਾਰਿਆ ਆਏ ਵਜਹੁ ਲਿਖਾਇ ॥ ਕਾਰ ਕਮਾਵਹਿ ਸਚ ਕੀ ਲਾਹਾ ਮਿਲੈ ਰਜਾਇ ॥ ਪੂੰਜੀ ਸਾਚੀ ਗੁਰੁ ਮਿਲੈ ਨਾ ਤਿਸੁ ਤਿਲੁ ਨ ਤਮਾਇ ॥੬॥
vāpārī vaṇjāri▫ā ā▫e vajahu likẖā▫e. Kār kamāvėh sacẖ kī lāhā milai rajā▫e. Pūnjī sācẖī gur milai nā ṯis ṯil na ṯamā▫e. ||6||

*(**Vanjaariaa**) travelling traders of (**vaapaari**) the business owner - the soul-merchants and traders - are born with their - tasks and - (**vajah-u**) emoluments preordained. They (**kamaavah-i**) carry out (**kaar**) the task (**ki**) of (**sach = truth**) truthfully complying with Divine commands, they (**milai**) receive (**rajaaey**) approval of union with God as (**laaha**) profit. They (**milai**) find the guru and become aware of (**saachi**) true (**poo'nji**) capital, i.e. remain reminded of Naam given by God; they have no (**til-u = mole on the skin**) fault and no (**tamaaey**) greed, i.e. are not attracted by other ideas. 6. M: 1, p 59.*

called court 'Dharam Rai' does this evaluation. He receives account of deeds of the creatures and examines them. The Paurri uses the concept of the weighing balance with two pans – the symbol of justice. The item to be weighed is put in one pan and weighing measure in the other. The latter is Naam/Divine commands and all deeds are tested against them.

ਅਮੁਲੁ ਧਰਮੁ ਅਮੁਲੁ ਦੀਬਾਣੁ ॥ ਅਮੁਲੁ ਤੁਲੁ ਅਮੁਲੁ ਪਰਵਾਣੁ ॥

Amul d̲h̲aram amul d̲ībāṇ. Amul t̲ul amul parvāṇ.

*(**Dharam-u = law**) the law/Naam by which they are judged is (**amul-u = priceless**) fair and (**deebaan-u**) the court/Dharam Rai is (**amul-u**) just.*
*(**Tul-u**) the weighing balance – having two pans has in one the priceless merchandise/conduct of the person and (**parvaan-u**) the weighing measure/Naam in the other, i.e. performance is evaluated against Naam/instructions for the role.*

ਅਮੁਲੁ ਬਖਸੀਸ ਅਮੁਲੁ ਨੀਸਾਣੁ ॥ ਅਮੁਲੁ ਕਰਮੁ ਅਮੁਲੁ ਫੁਰਮਾਣੁ ॥

Amul bakẖsīs amul nīsāṇ. Amul karam amul furmāṇ.

*Those who conform to Naam receive (**amul-u**) the priceless (**neesaan-u**) mark of priceless (**bakhsees**) Divine grace.*
*(**Karam-u**) Divine grace is priceless and (**phurmaan-u = order**) decision of the Almighty is priceless/just.*

The Paurri further says we may try but it is not possible to describe the Master:

ਅਮੁਲੋ ਅਮੁਲੁ ਆਖਿਆ ਨ ਜਾਇ ॥ ਆਖਿ ਆਖਿ ਰਹੇ ਲਿਵ ਲਾਇ ॥

Amulo amul ākẖi▫ā na jā▫e. Ākẖ ākẖ rahe liv lā▫e

*(**Amulo**) the priceless Almighty (**amul-u = beyond price**) beyond measure and (**na jaaey**) cannot be (**aakhiaa = told**) described.*
*Many (**rahey**) keep (**liv**) attention (**laaey**) fixed/contemplate and try to (**aakh-i**) state them, i.e. praise the Almighty.*

Paurri 26 Part 2.

The second part of Paurri 26 mentions that numerous entities praise the Almighty. Some people read the scriptures and give discourses. Some do it through worshipping gods and goddesses but not realizing that even the latter praise the Divine. No description is complete:

ਆਖਹਿ ਵੇਦ ਪਾਠ ਪੁਰਾਣ ॥ ਆਖਹਿ ਪੜੇ ਕਰਹਿ ਵਖਿਆਣ ॥
Ākẖahi veḏ pāṯẖ purāṇ. Ākẖahi paṛe karahi vakẖiāṇ.

*Some (**aakhah-i**) say (**paatth**) by reading (**veyd**) the Vedas and (**puraan**) Puranas, i.e. the scriptures.*
*Some who (**parrey**) have read the scriptures, (**karah-i = make**) give (**vakhiaan**) discourses on greatness of the Almighty.*

ਆਖਹਿ ਬਰਮੇ ਆਖਹਿ ਇੰਦ ॥ ਆਖਹਿ ਗੋਪੀ ਤੈ ਗੋਵਿੰਦ ॥
Ākẖahi barme ākẖahi inḏ. Ākẖahi gopī ṯai govinḏ.

*Numerous gods like (**barmey**) Brahmas and (**ind**) Indras – whom people worship - (**aakhah-i**) praise and obey the Almighty. The stories of (**gopee**) the milkmaids (**tai**) and (**govind = master of cows**) Krishna in the Mahabharata represent the Creator's play.*

ਆਖਹਿ ਈਸਰ ਆਖਹਿ ਸਿਧ ॥ ਆਖਹਿ ਕੇਤੇ ਕੀਤੇ ਬੁਧ ॥
Ākẖahi īsar ākẖahi siḏẖ. Ākẖahi keṯe kīṯe buḏẖ

Numerous ***(eesar)*** *Shankar/Shiva* ***(aakhah-i)*** *praise as do* ***(sidh)*** *the yogis.* ***(Ketey = as many)*** *all* ***(budh)*** *the Buddhas/wise people* ***(keetey)*** *created by the Almighty* ***(aakhah-i = say)*** *acknowledge allegiance to the Almighty.*

ਆਖਹਿ ਦਾਨਵ ਆਖਹਿ ਦੇਵ ॥ ਆਖਹਿ ਸੁਰਿ ਨਰ ਮੁਨਿ ਜਨ ਸੇਵ ॥

Ākẖahi ḏānav ākẖahi ḏev. Ākẖahi sur nar mun jan sev.

Both ***(daanav)*** *the demons and* ***(deyv)*** *gods* ***(aakhah-i)*** *praise God; as do* ***(sur-i nar)*** *godly persons,* ***(mun-i)*** *sages and* ***(jan = servants, seyv = servants)*** *the devotees/seekers.*

ਕੇਤੇ ਆਖਹਿ ਆਖਣਿ ਪਾਹਿ ॥ ਕੇਤੇ ਕਹਿ ਕਹਿ ਉਠਿ ਉਠਿ ਜਾਹਿ ॥

Keṯe ākẖahi ākẖaṇ pāhi. Keṯe kahi kahi uṯẖ uṯẖ jāhi.

(Keytey = as many) *numerous persons* ***(aakhah-i = say)*** *praise and* ***(aakhan-i paah-i)*** *keep praising.* ***(Keytey)*** *numerous person* ***(kah-i kah-i)*** *keep praising until they* ***(utth-i utth-i jaah-i)*** *depart, i.e. until death.*

ਏਤੇ ਕੀਤੇ ਹੋਰਿ ਕਰੇਹਿ ॥ ਤਾ ਆਖਿ ਨ ਸਕਹਿ ਕੇਈ ਕੇਇ ॥

Ėṯe kīṯe hor karehi. Ŧā ākẖ na sakahi ke▫ī ke▫e.

The Creator ***(keetey)*** *created* ***(eytey)*** *these many and if IT* ***(karah-i)*** *creates* ***(hor-i)*** *more; even* ***(ta)*** *then* ***(na keyee key-i = not any)*** *no one* ***(sakah-i)*** *can* ***(aakh-i = say)*** *describe virtues and powers of the Almighty.*

ਜੇਵਡੁ ਭਾਵੈ ਤੇਵਡੁ ਹੋਇ ॥ ਨਾਨਕ ਜਾਣੈ ਸਾਚਾ ਸੋਇ

Jevad bẖāvai ṯevad ho▫e. Nānak jāṇai sācẖā so▫e

*The Almighty can (**hoey**) become (**teyvadd-u**) that great (**jeyvadd-u**) as great IT (**bhaavai**) likes, i.e. gives understanding as IT pleases; (**soey = that one**) the One (**saachaa**) Eternal Master alone (**jaanai**) knows Divine greatness, says Guru Nanak.*

ਜੇ ਕੋ ਆਖੈ ਬੋਲੁਵਿਗਾੜੁ ॥ ਤਾ ਲਿਖੀਐ ਸਿਰਿ ਗਾਵਾਰਾ ਗਾਵਾਰੁ ॥੨੬॥

Je ko ākẖai boluvigāṛ. Ŧā likī▫ai sir gāvārā gāvār. ||26||

*(**Jey**) if (**ko**) someone (**aakhah-i**) says this (**boluvigaarr-u**) twisted – alludes this capability to the self; (**ta**) then s/he is (**likheeai**) is written in the list as (**gavaar-u**) a fool (**sir-i = over the head**) above (**gaavaara**) all fools. 26.*

<u>Paurri 27</u>

Paurri 27 brings out the harmony in existence with all components of the universe performing their functions in a mutually supporting manner. It is like components of a musical group, play music and sing in unison. The Creator, the director of this show is unseen; the seeker wishing to have vision of the Creator asks:

ਸੋ ਦਰੁ ਕੇਹਾ ਸੋ ਘਰੁ ਕੇਹਾ ਜਿਤੁ ਬਹਿ ਸਰਬ ਸਮਾਲੇ ॥

So ḏar kehā so gẖar kehā jiṯ bahi sarab samāle.

*(**Keyha = what type**) which is that (**dar**) seat and (**ghar = house**) place where you (**bah-i**) sit and (**samaaley = take care**) direct all activity, o Creator?*

ਵਾਜੇ ਨਾਦ ਅਨੇਕ ਅਸੰਖਾ ਕੇਤੇ ਵਾਵਣਹਾਰੇ ॥ ਕੇਤੇ ਰਾਗ ਪਰੀ ਸਿਉ ਕਹੀਅਨਿ ਕੇਤੇ ਗਾਵਣਹਾਰੇ ॥

vāje nāḏ anek asankẖā keṯe vāvaṇhāre. Keṯe rāg parī si▫o kahī▫an keṯe gāvaṇhāre.

There are ***(aneyk = numerous, asankha = countless)*** *innumerable* ***(vaajey)*** *musical instruments producing different* ***(naad)*** *sounds and* ***(keytey)*** *numerous* ***(vaavan-haarey)*** *players playing them.*

There are ***(ketey)*** *numerous* ***(gaavan-haarey)*** *singers* ***(kaheean-i = saying)*** *singing* ***(siau)*** *to* ***(ketey)*** *numerous* ***(raag)*** *ragas and* ***(pari = wives of ragas)*** *raginis/sub-ragas.*

Note 1: This is an interesting analogy. The music composer composes the music, the musical instruments play that music and the singers sing to it. The music director directs them. In the universe, the Creator made the cosmic laws. The sun, earth and the moon together produce the phenomena of day/night, seasons, and lunar cycles. The creatures' activities accord with these phenomena like working during day and resting at night. Here the Creator is the music composer as well as the director; sun, earth and the moon, which cause seasons, days of the week, lit or dark nights, day and night are the musical instruments, and the creatures are the singers. The cosmic laws represent the ragas or the musical patterns to which the instruments play and singers sing, i.e. play their roles according to Divine commands/cosmic laws.

Note 2: The verses below show that singing praises is acknowledging and obeying the Master. The message is that elements like air, water and fire perform their roles; human beings should carry out their duties.

Note 3: Dharam Rai mentioned is the metaphorical judge in the Divine Court who evaluates the creatures' deeds. 'Chitra Gupt' the unseen metaphorical recorders keep record of the deeds, which Dharam Rai considers. This means the system judges everyone justly, based on their deeds.

ਗਾਵਹਿ ਤੁਹਨੋ ਪਉਣੁ ਪਾਣੀ ਬੈਸੰਤਰੁ ਗਾਵੈ ਰਾਜਾ ਧਰਮੁ ਦੁਆਰੇ ॥ ਗਾਵਹਿ ਚਿਤੁ ਗੁਪਤੁ ਲਿਖਿ ਜਾਣਹਿ ਲਿਖਿ ਲਿਖਿ ਧਰਮੁ ਵੀਚਾਰੇ ॥

Gāvahi ṯuhno pa▫uṇ pāṇī baisanṯar gāvai rājā ḏẖaram ḏu▫āre. Gāvahi cẖiṯ gupaṯ likẖ jāṇėh likẖ likẖ ḏẖaram vīcẖāre.

*O Creator, (**pavan**) air, (**paanee**) water and (**baisantar**) fire (**gaavah-i = sing**) praise/obey (**tuhno**) You, as (**gaavai = sings**) does Dharam Rai the metaphorical judge to present facts in Your (**duaarey**) court.*
*Chit-u/Chitra Gupt-u the metaphorical Divine recorder (**gaavah-i = sing**) watches and writes, and the Divine judge (**dharam-u**) Dharam Rai (**beecharey**) considers (**likh-i likh-i**) what is written, metaphorically speaking.*

Note 4: It would be noticed that whereas with all other entities 'Gaavah-i' meaning 'they sing' has been used it is 'Gaavai' meaning 'sings' in the case of 'Dharam'. That is because others are multiple in number and Dharam Rai is one and hence a singular term is used.

Note 5: The next set of entities is of the Hindu gods and goddesses, who are believed to be doing God's bidding. Hindu beliefs revolve round these entities. Their inclusion here shows that while the mortals worship them, they themselves acknowledge the Eternal. They perform their roles as directed by the Creator.

ਗਾਵਹਿ ਈਸਰੁ ਬਰਮਾ ਦੇਵੀ ਸੋਹਨਿ ਸਦਾ ਸਵਾਰੇ ॥ ਗਾਵਹਿ ਇੰਦ ਇਦਾਸਣਿ ਬੈਠੇ ਦੇਵਤਿਆ ਦਰਿ ਨਾਲੇ ॥

Gāvahi īsar barmā devī sohan sadā savāre.Gāvahi ind idāsaṇ baithe deviti◌ā dar nāle.

*(**Eesar**) Shankar/Mahadev/Shiva, Brahma and (**deyvee**) the goddess (**gaavah-i = sing**) acknowledge You as the Master; they (**sohan = lookg ood**) are respected because they have been (**savaarey**) adorned by You i.e. their concepts are created by You.*
*(**Baitthey**) sitting on (**indaasan-i**) the seat/throne of Indra, (**ind**) Indras – the kings of gods - (**gaavah-i**) praise You (**naaley**) along-with all the gods sitting (**dar-i**) in his court.*

Note 6: The Guru says next that all those respected on the earth also owe their positions to devotion to the Divine:

ਗਾਵਹਿ ਸਿਧ ਸਮਾਧੀ ਅੰਦਰਿ ਗਾਵਨਿ ਸਾਧ ਵਿਚਾਰੇ ॥ ਗਾਵਨਿ ਜਤੀ ਸਤੀ ਸੰਤੋਖੀ ਗਾਵਹਿ ਵੀਰ ਕਰਾਰੇ ॥

Gāvahi sidh samādhī andar gāvan sādh vichāre. Gāvan jatī satī santokhī gāvahi vīr karāre.

*(**Sidh**) the accomplished saints sitting (**andar**) in (**samaadhi**) meditation acknowledge You as do (**saadh**) the seekers (**vichaarey**) in contemplation.*
*(**Jatee**) the celibates, (**satee**) donors, (**santokhee**) the contented ones – those happy with Divine will - and (**kraarey**) the strong (**veer**) warriors acknowledge You i.e. they have been given these roles and ability by You.*

ਗਾਵਨਿ ਪੰਡਿਤ ਪੜਨਿ ਰਖੀਸਰ ਜੁਗੁ ਜੁਗੁ ਵੇਦਾ ਨਾਲੇ ॥ ਗਾਵਹਿ ਮੋਹਣੀਆ ਮਨੁ ਮੋਹਨਿ ਸੁਰਗਾ ਮਛ ਪਇਆਲੇ ॥

Gāvan pandiṯ paṛan rakẖīsar jug jug veḏā nāle. Gāvahi mohṇī▫ā man mohan surgā macẖẖ pa▫i▫āle

*(**Pandit**) the learned scholars who (**parran-i**) read scriptures and (**rakheesur**) the great sages (**gaavah-i**) praise You (**jug jug = age after age**) forever (**naaley = with**) according to (**veydaa**) the teachings of the Vedas/scriptures*[1].
*(**Mohneea**) captivating beautiful women who (**mohan**) fascinate (**man**) the mind, (**gaavah-i = sing**) acknowledge, i.e. owe their beauty to, You; as do (**surag**) heaven, (**machh**) the world and (**paiaaley**) the nether regions.*

Note 7: According to Hindu mythology, the gods and demons together churned the ocean, which brought out fourteen jewels, things of great value. Also, the Hindus believe there are sixty eight pilgrim centres and one is purified by bathing there:

ਗਾਵਨਿ ਰਤਨ ਉਪਾਏ ਤੇਰੇ ਅਠਸਠਿ ਤੀਰਥ ਨਾਲੇ ॥

Gāvan raṯan upā▫e ṯere aṯẖsaṯẖ ṯirath nāle

*The mythological fourteen (**ratan**) jewels (**naaley**) along-with (**atth-satth**) the sixty eight (**teerath**) places of Hindu Pilgrimage acknowledge you - i.e. the devotees visit them to find You.*

---

[1] In Aasa Di Vaar, the second Slok/prologue preceding Paurri 13, Guru Nanak gives this linkage between the Vedas and Jug/ages: Saam Veda – Satyug when only the pristine Almighty was praised. Later the linkge is Rama/Treyta Yug with Rig Veda, Krishna/Duaapar Yug with Yajur Veda and Kaliyg with Atharv Veda.

Note 8: A story about churning the ocean appears in the texts Bhagavata Purana, the Mahabharata and the Vishnu Purana according to which gods and demons churned the ocean and brought out fourteen Ratan or jewels, i.e. persons and things of value. Like all Puraanic stories, this is metaphorical. The fourteen Ratan or jewels were as follows:

The fourteen Ratan or jewels were as follows:

1. Chandra' (Moon).
2. 'Parijat', a tree in the Paradise of Indra.
3. 'Airavat', a multi-tusked elephant of Indra.
4. 'Kamadhenu', a cow which fulfils wishes.
5. 'Uchchaihsravas' the white horse of Indra.
6. 'Sankha' the conch of Lord Vishnu used for victory.
7. 'Gada' or mace.
8. 'Laxmi', goddess of wealth.
9. 'Rambha', the apsara (celestial beauty) in heaven.
10. 'Ratnas', (gems and jewel).
11. 'Kalpavriksha', a wish-fulfilling
12. 'Dhanwantari', the physician for all Gods.
13. 'Mada', a goddess
14. 'Amrit' (the nectar drinking which one becomes immortal) in a golden chalice (Kumbha/vessel).

(Source: Web page Samudra Manthan and 14 Ratnas).

The above list is for information. It has no spiritual significance in Sikh thought. The Paurri clearly says God has created these Ratans/jewels. The Gurbani teaching on the subject is that churning of the sea should be taken as searching the mind to find God, and be aware of Divine virtues and commands with the guru's guidance[1].

---

[1] Paurri 6 stated:

ਗਾਵਹਿ ਜੋਧ ਮਹਾਬਲ ਸੂਰਾ ਗਾਵਹਿ ਖਾਣੀ ਚਾਰੇ ॥

Gāvahi jodẖ mahābal sūrā gāvahi kẖāṇī cẖāre.

*All the (**mahaabal = powerful**) great (**jodh**) warriors and (**soora**) the brave ones acknowledge You, as do (**chaarey**) all the four ways of creating (**khaanee**) life forms – namely Andaj – from egg/birds, Jeyraj = from womb/mammals, Seytaj – from perspiration/ticks, Utbhuj – from soil/worms and plants.*

Note 9: The next set of entities are those held in space by according to cosmic laws:

ਗਾਵਹਿ ਖੰਡ ਮੰਡਲ ਵਰਭੰਡਾ ਕਰਿ ਕਰਿ ਰਖੇ ਧਾਰੇ ॥

Gāvahi kẖand mandal varbẖandā kar kar rakẖe ḏẖāre.

*(**Khandd**) the planets, (**mandal**) galaxies and (**varbhanddaa/brahmandd**) universes created and (**rakhey**) placed in space acknowledge You – conform to Divine commands i.e. cosmic laws.*

ਸੇਈ ਤੁਧੁਨੋ ਗਾਵਹਿ ਜੋ ਤੁਧੁ ਭਾਵਨਿ ਰਤੇ ਤੇਰੇ ਭਗਤ ਰਸਾਲੇ ॥

Se▫ī ṯuḏẖuno gāvahi jo ṯuḏẖ bẖāvan raṯe ṯere bẖagaṯ rasāle.

ਮਤਿ ਵਿਚਿ ਰਤਨ ਜਵਾਹਰ ਮਾਣਿਕ ਜੇ ਇਕ ਗੁਰ ਕੀ ਸਿਖ ਸੁਣੀ ॥

Maṯ vicẖ raṯan javāhar māṇik je ik gur kī sikẖ suṇī.

*(**Ratan, javaahar, maanik = precious stones**) jewels and gems of awareness of Naam/Divine virtues and commands - are present (**vich-i**) in the (**mat-i = intellect**) human mind – and one becomes aware of them - (**jey**) if one (**suni**) listens to (**sikh**) the teachings (**ki**) of (**ik-u = one**) the true guru.*

*O Almighty, (**Seyee**) only those (**jo**) who (**bhaavan**) are liked by (**tudh-u**) You, i.e. whom you motivate, (**gaavan = sing**) praise/obey You; (**bhagat**) devotees (**teyrey**) of Yours are (**ratey**) imbued with your love and (**rasaaley**) relish it.*

ਹੋਰਿ ਕੇਤੇ ਗਾਵਨਿ ਸੇ ਮੈ ਚਿਤਿ ਨ ਆਵਨਿ ਨਾਨਕੁ ਕਿਆ ਵੀਚਾਰੇ ॥

Hor kete gāvan se mai chit na āvan Nānak ki▫ā vīchāre.

*(**Keytey**) how many (**hor-i**) more who (**gaavan**) praise You but (**sey**) they do not (**aavan**) come to (**mai**) my (**chit**) mind i.e. they are beyond count and Nanak (**kia = how, veechaarey = think**) cannot express any view of them, i.e. it is hard to know the entire creation.*

Note 10. All entities mentioned above are created and perishable, but the Creator is neither created nor perishable, says the next verse.

ਸੋਈ ਸੋਈ ਸਦਾ ਸਚੁ ਸਾਹਿਬੁ ਸਾਚਾ ਸਾਚੀ ਨਾਈ ॥ ਹੈ ਭੀ ਹੋਸੀ ਜਾਇ ਨ ਜਾਸੀ ਰਚਨਾ ਜਿਨਿ ਰਚਾਈ ॥

So▫ī so▫ī sadā sach sāhib sāchā sāchī nā▫ī. Hai bhī hosī jā▫e na jāsī rachnā jin rachā▫ī.

*(**Soee soee = only that**) there is only one (**sach-u**) Eternal (**sahib-u**) Master (**sadaa**) forever, and (**naaee**) Naam/writ of (**saacha**) the Eternal applies (**saachee**) forever; the creation is perishable but the Creator who (**rachaai**) made it (**hai**) is present now, (**bhee hosee**) shall also be and (**jaaey na jaasi**) shall not perish now or later i.e. is Eternal.*

ਰੰਗੀ ਰੰਗੀ ਭਾਤੀ ਕਰਿ ਕਰਿ ਜਿਨਸੀ ਮਾਇਆ ਜਿਨਿ ਉਪਾਈ ॥ ਕਰਿ ਕਰਿ ਵੇਖੈ ਕੀਤਾ ਆਪਣਾ ਜਿਵ ਤਿਸ ਦੀ ਵਡਿਆਈ ॥

Rangī rangī bẖāṯī kar kar jinsī mā▫i▫ā jin upā▫ī. Kar kar vekẖai kīṯā āpṇā jiv ṯis ḏī vadi▫ā▫ī.

It is the Creator ***(jin-i)*** *who* ***(kar-i kar-i)*** *made* ***(rachna)*** *the creation* ***(range rangee)*** *of different hues and in numerous* ***(bhaatee)*** *types as* ***(maaiaa/maya)*** *world-play IT* ***(kar-i kar-i)*** *creates and* ***(deykhai)*** *watches the creation;* ***(jiv = as)*** *this is* ***(tis = that, di = of)*** *God's* ***(vaddiaaee)*** *greatness - who is both the Creator and Sustainor*[1]*.*

ਜੋ ਤਿਸੁ ਭਾਵੈ ਸੋਈ ਕਰਸੀ ਹੁਕਮੁ ਨ ਕਰਣਾ ਜਾਈ ॥ ਸੋ ਪਾਤਿਸਾਹੁ ਸਾਹਾ ਪਾਤਿਸਾਹਿਬੁ ਨਾਨਕ ਰਹਣੁ ਰਜਾਈ ॥੨੭॥

Jo ṯis bẖāvai so▫ī karsī hukam na karṇā jā▫ī. So pāṯisāhu sāhā pāṯisāhib Nānak rahaṇ rajā▫ī. ||27||

The Creator ***(karsi)*** *does* ***(jo)*** *what* ***(bhaavai)*** *pleases* ***(tis-u)*** *IT, i.e. everything happens systemically according to cosmic laws; no one* ***(jaaee)*** *can* ***(karna)*** *give* ***(hukam-u)*** *orders on how the universe should function.*

---

[1] This is restated later in Paurri 31 thus:

ਕਰਿ ਕਰਿ ਵੇਖੈ ਸਿਰਜਣਹਾਰੁ ॥ ਨਾਨਕ ਸਚੇ ਕੀ ਸਾਚੀ ਕਾਰ ॥

Kar kar vekẖai sirjaṇhār. Nānak sacẖe kī sācẖī kār.

(Sirjanhaar-u) *the Creator* ***(kar-i)*** *creates and* ***(kar-i)*** *having created* ***(veykhai)*** *watches – looks after and supervises/evaluates.*
This is not an illusion; ***(kaar)*** *work of* ***(sachey = true)*** *real Master is* ***(saachi)*** *real – not metaphor, says Guru Nanak.*

*(**So** = **that**) the Almighty (**paatisahib-u**) Supreme Master is (**saahu**) the Master of (**paatsaahu**) the Emperors; everyone and everything (**rahan-u** = **live**) exists (**rajaaee** = **will**) the Divine writ/cosmic laws. 27.*

Preface to Paurris 28-31.

One of the more vocal groups present at the time of Guru Nanak were the Yogis who tried to get the Guru join them. He had long discussions with them, which are recorded, in his composition Sidh Gosatt meaning dialogue with the Yogis. He noticed and pointed out that the Yogis were only engaging in symbolism. They also tried to impress the Guru by showing miracles. In Paurris 28 to 31, the Guru takes these symbols one by one and gives practical meaning for each. All the four Paurris end with:

ਆਦੇਸੁ ਤਿਸੈ ਆਦੇਸੁ ॥ ਆਦਿ ਅਨੀਲੁ ਅਨਾਦਿ ਅਨਾਹਤਿ ਜੁਗੁ ਜੁਗੁ ਏਕੋ ਵੇਸੁ ॥

Āḏes ṯisai āḏes. Āḏ anīl anāḏ anāhaṯ jug jug eko ves.

*My (**aadeys-u**) salutation and obeisance is (**tisai** = **that**) to the One,*

*Who is (**aad-i**) the beginning of all but IT-self (**anaad-i**) without a beginning, (**aneel-u** = **not blue/coloured**) touched and (**eyko** = **one, veys** = **garb/state**) is in the same (**jug-u jug-u**) from age to age.*

Note: The pronoun 'IT' has been used for God who is not a person and is gender-neutral.

Paurri 28

ਮੁੰਦਾ ਸੰਤੋਖੁ ਸਰਮੁ ਪਤੁ ਝੋਲੀ ਧਿਆਨ ਕੀ ਕਰਹਿ ਬਿਭੂਤਿ ॥ ਖਿੰਥਾ ਕਾਲੁ ਕੁਆਰੀ ਕਾਇਆ ਜੁਗਤਿ ਡੰਡਾ ਪਰਤੀਤਿ ॥

Munḏa sanṯokẖ saram paṯ jẖolī ḏẖi▫ān kī karahi bibẖūṯ. Kẖinthā kāl ku▫ārī kā▫i▫ā jugaṯ dandā parṯīṯ.

*The yogi pierces the ears and wears (**munda**) earrings as symbol for contentment - but one overcomes desires by happily accepting and obeying by Divine commands/natural laws.*
*Instead of carrying (**pat-u**) a bowl and (**jholi**) bag for begging food items as the yogi does, one should (**saram-u**) work hard to make a living.*
*Instead of the yogi smearing the body with ash as sign of humility, he should humbly (**karah-i**) apply (**bibhoot-i**) the ash (**ki**) of, humbly (**dhiaan**) paying attention/obedience to Divine commands, i.e. kill ego and obey the Almighty.*
*One should be conscious of (**kaal-u**) death – and not get attached to the world-play - rather than wear (**khintha**) a garment made of rags as symbol.*
*Keeping (**kaaiaa = body**) the self (**kuaaree = virgin**) untouched by vices, is (**jugat-i = method**) the way to find the Almighty.*
*The Yogi carries (**ddandaa**) a staff to show control over the self but one achieves this by (**parteet-i**) remaining conscious of Divine virtues and commands.*

Note: There are twelve tribes of Yogis and most of them are in conflict with one another. One of them, called Aaee Panth, has no conflict with any other. This happens by purifying the mind of jealousy. Paurri 28 says: One, who has conquered the mind, can conquer the world.

ਆਈ ਪੰਥੀ ਸਗਲ ਜਮਾਤੀ ਮਨਿ ਜੀਤੈ ਜਗੁ ਜੀਤੁ ॥

Āªī panthī sagal jamāṯī man jīṯai jag jīṯ.

*One should be (**sagal = all, jamaati = of classes**) friendly to everyone rather than just being Aaee Panthi, i.e. belong to the friendly yogi tribe Aaee. Being friendly comes (**jeetai**) by conquering the mind from ego; and one who does that can (**jeet-u**) conquer (**jag-u**) the world, i.e. one who drives evil out of mind is liked by everyone[1].*

ਆਦੇਸੁ ਤਿਸੈ ਆਦੇਸੁ ॥ ਆਦਿ ਅਨੀਲੁ ਅਨਾਦਿ ਅਨਾਹਤਿ ਜੁਗੁ ਜੁਗੁ ਏਕੋ ਵੇਸੁ ॥੨੮॥

Āḏes ṯisai āḏes. Āḏ anīl anāḏ anāhaṯ jug jug eko ves. ||28||

*Our (**aadeys-u**) salutation and (**aadeys-u**) obeisance should be (**tisai = to that one**) to the One Almighty.*

*Who is (**aad-i**) the beginning of all but IT-self (**anaad-i**) without a beginning, (**aneel-u = without blue colour/without colour**) un-stained i.e. free from worldly influence, (**anaahat-i**) indestructible and (**eyko = one, veys = garb/form**) unchanging (**jug-u jug-u**) from age to age. 28.*

<u>Paurri 29.</u>

---

[1] Sukhmani Sahib says: ਮਨ ਅਪੁਨੇ ਤੇ ਬੁਰਾ ਮਿਟਾਨਾ ॥ਪੇਖੈ ਸਗਲ ਸ੍ਰਿਸਟਿ ਸਾਜਨਾ ॥
Man apune ṯe burā mitānā. Pekẖai sagal sarisat sājnā.

*One who looks within, understands that in most cases one can trace the responsibility for a conflict situation to the self. By (**mitaana**) removing (**bura**) evil (**tey**) from (**apney**) from one's own (**man**) mind,*
*one (**pekhai**) sees (**sagal**) the whole (**sristt-i = universe**) all creatures as (**saajna**) friends and no adversaries. M; 5, 266.*

Note: The Yogis organise Bhanddaaras, i.e. large feasts offering to God and distribute it. They play ਸਿੰਙੀ Singni – which produces trumpet-like Naad/sound to announce distribution of food. They try to show miracles. They believe that these connect them to God. Paurri 29 below comments on these.

ਭੁਗਤਿ ਗਿਆਨੁ ਦਇਆ ਭੰਡਾਰਣਿ ਘਟਿ ਘਟਿ ਵਾਜਹਿ ਨਾਦ ॥

Bẖugaṯ gi▫ān ḏa▫i▫ā bẖandāraṇ gẖat gẖat vājėh nāḏ.

*(**Bhugat-i**) food sustains the body; similarly (**giaan-u**) awareness of Naam sustains the mind in the midst of temptations; this awareness comes with (**daiaa**) kindness of the guru (**bhaddaaran-i = storekeeper/distributor**) who imparts Giaan-u/awareness of Naam/Divine commands. (**Naad-i = sound/music**) celestial music (**vaajah-i**) plays/Divine messages are received (**ghatt-i ghatt-**i) in every mind – the guru enlightens the mind to experience this.*

ਆਪਿ ਨਾਥੁ ਨਾਥੀ ਸਭ ਜਾ ਕੀ ਰਿਧਿ ਸਿਧਿ ਅਵਰਾ ਸਾਦ ॥ ਸੰਜੋਗੁ ਵਿਜੋਗੁ ਦੁਇ ਕਾਰ ਚਲਾਵਹਿ ਲੇਖੇ ਆਵਹਿ ਭਾਗ ॥

Āp nāth nāthī sabẖ jā kī riḏẖ siḏẖ avrā sāḏ. Sanjog vijog ḏu▫e kār cẖalāvėh lekẖe āvahi bẖāg.

*(**Aap-i = self**) the Creator is (**naath-u**) the Master (**ja ki**) in whose (**naathee = leashed at the nose – as some animals are**) control (**sabh**) all are, i.e. everything happens by Divine commands/cosmic laws.*

*(**Ridh-i sidh-i**) miraculous practices are (**avraa = other**)*

*of different (**saad**) taste, i.e. they are adopted due to ego to impress people – and are obstacles in way of union with God.*

*Past influences (**chalavah-i**) drive the soul on (**kaar = tasks**) path either of (**sanjog-u**) union with, or (**vijog-u = separation**) remaining away from, the Creator; one's (**bhaag**) deeds are (**aavah-i = come**) taken into (**leykhai**) account for the decision for this.*

ਆਦੇਸੁ ਤਿਸੈ ਆਦੇਸੁ ॥ ਆਦਿ ਅਨੀਲੁ ਅਨਾਦਿ ਅਨਾਹਤਿ ਜੁਗੁ ਜੁਗੁ ਏਕੋ ਵੇਸੁ ॥੨੯॥

Āḏes ṯisai āḏes. Āḏ anīl anāḏ anāhaṯ jug jug eko ves. ||29||

*Our (**aadeys-u**) salutation and (**aadeys-u**) obeisance should be (**tisai = to that one**) to the One Almighty.*

*Who is (**aad-i**) the beginning of all but IT-self (**anaad-i**) without a beginning, (**aneel-u = without blue color/without color**) un-stained i.e. free from worldly influence, (**anaahat-i**) indestructible and (**eyko = one, veys = garb/form**) unchanging (**jug-u jug-u**) from age to age. 29.*

Note: According to Hindu mythology, three gods manage all creation with Brahma as the creator, Vishnu as the sustainer and Mahesh/Shiva delivers justice. Paurri 30 calls this as illusory, and explains:

Paurri 30.

ਏਕਾ ਮਾਈ ਜੁਗਤਿ ਵਿਆਈ ਤਿਨਿ ਚੇਲੇ ਪਰਵਾਣੁ ॥ ਇਕੁ ਸੰਸਾਰੀ ਇਕੁ ਭੰਡਾਰੀ ਇਕੁ ਲਾਏ ਦੀਬਾਣੁ ॥

Ėkā mā▫ī jugaṯ vi▫ā▫ī ṯin cẖele parvāṇ. Ik sansārī ik bẖandārī ik lā▫e ḏībāṇ.

*It is (**parvaan-u**) accepted/believed that (**eyka**) the One Almighty (**jugat-i = method**) caused an illusory (**maaee**) mother (**viaaee**) to produce (**tin-i**) three (**cheyley**) disciples/servants, i.e. the Almighty created the illusion of three gods.*

*(**Ik-u**) one of them Brahma is creator (**sansaaree**) of the world; Vishnu is (**bhanddaaree = store-holder**) provider/sustainer and Mahesh/Shiva (**laaey**) holds (**deebaan-u**) court, i.e. takes account of deeds of the creatures and administers justice.*

ਜਿਵ ਤਿਸੁ ਭਾਵੈ ਤਿਵੈ ਚਲਾਵੈ ਜਿਵ ਹੋਵੈ ਫੁਰਮਾਣੁ ॥ ਓਹੁ ਵੇਖੈ ਓਨਾ ਨਦਰਿ ਨ ਆਵੈ ਬਹੁਤਾ ਏਹੁ ਵਿਡਾਣੁ ॥

Jiv ṯis bẖāvai ṯivai cẖalāvai jiv hovai furmāṇ. Oh vekẖai onā naḏar na āvai bahuṯā ehu vidāṇ.

They do not act on their own. *(**Jiv**) as (**tis-u = that**) the Almighty (**bhaavai**) likes/decides, IT (**chalaavai = drives**) causes things to happen (**tivai**) that way; (**jiv**) as is (**phurmaan-u**) the Divine command/writ, i.e. everything happens by Divine commands/cosmic laws naturally.*

*(**Oh = that**) the Almighty (**veykhai**) watches, i.e. knows what goes on, but nothing (**aavai = comes, nadar-i = in sight**) is seen (**ona**) by them; (**eyh-u**) this is (**bahutaa**) the big (**viddaan-u**) difference, i.e. the Almighty is real and they are illusory – things happen by Divine will.*

ਆਦੇਸੁ ਤਿਸੈ ਆਦੇਸੁ ॥ ਆਦਿ ਅਨੀਲੁ ਅਨਾਦਿ ਅਨਾਹਤਿ ਜੁਗੁ ਜੁਗੁ ਏਕੋ ਵੇਸੁ ॥ ੩੦॥

Āḏes ṯisai āḏes. Āḏ anīl anāḏ anāhaṯ jug jug eko ves. ||30||

Our ***(aadeys-u)*** *salutation and* ***(aadeys-u)*** *obeisance should be* ***(tisai = to that one)*** *to the One Almighty.*
Who is ***(aad-i)*** *the beginning of all but IT-self* ***(anaad-i)*** *without a beginning,* ***(aneel-u = without blue colour/without colour)*** *un-stained i.e. free from worldly influence,* ***(anaahat-i)*** *indestructible and* ***(eyko = one, veys = garb/form)*** *unchanging* ***(jug-u jug-u)*** *from age to. 30.*

Note: The Yogis believe Shiva has Aasan/seat and provisions in Shiv Lok. That is a limited perception. The creatures in the jungle, on mountains, under the rocks, in water, on land are made the wherewithal provided there, by the Creator, before they are born. They however need to make effort to get it. Man has provided nothing new; s/he only keeps discovering more and more.

Paurri 31.

ਆਸਣੁ ਲੋਇ ਲੋਇ ਭੰਡਾਰ ॥ ਜੋ ਕਿਛੁ ਪਾਇਆ ਸੁ ਏਕਾ ਵਾਰ ॥
Āsaṇ lo▫e lo▫e bẖandār. Jo kicẖẖ pā▫i▫ā so ekā vār.

The Almighty has ***(aasan-u)*** *seat/presence and* ***(bhanddaar)*** *stores/provisions* ***(loey loey)*** *in every habitat. Whatever is needed* ***(su)*** *that* ***(paaiaa)*** *has been put* ***(eyka vaar = one time)*** *once for all.*

ਕਰਿ ਕਰਿ ਵੇਖੈ ਸਿਰਜਣਹਾਰੁ ॥ ਨਾਨਕ ਸਚੇ ਕੀ ਸਾਚੀ ਕਾਰ ॥
Kar kar vekẖai sirjaṇhār. Nānak sacẖe kī sācẖī kār.

(Sirjanhaar-u) *the Creator* ***(kar-i)*** *creates and* ***(kar-i)*** *having created* ***(veykhai)*** *watches – looks after and supervises/evaluates.*
This is not an illusion; ***(kaar)*** *work of* ***(sachey = true)*** *real Master is* ***(saachi)*** *real, says Guru Nanak.*

ਆਾਦੇਸੁ ਤਿਸੈ ਆਾਦੇਸੁ ॥ ਆਦਿ ਅਨੀਲੁ ਅਨਾਦਿ ਅਨਾਹਤਿ ਜੁਗੁ ਜੁਗੁ ਏਕੋ ਵੇਸੁ ॥੩੧॥

Ādes tisai ādes. Ād anīl anād anāhat jug jug eko ves. ||31||

Our ***(aadeys-u)*** *salutation and* ***(aadeys-u)*** *obeisance should be* ***(tisai = to that one)*** *to the One Almighty.*
Who is ***(aad-i)*** *the beginning of all but IT-self* ***(anaad-i)*** *without a beginning,* ***(aneel-u = without blue color/without color)*** *un-stained i.e. free from worldly influence,* ***(anaahat-i)*** *indestructible and* ***(eyko = one, veys = garb/form)*** *unchanging* ***(jug-u jug-u)*** *from age to age. 31.*

Preface to Paurris 32-33

The creature's soul yearns to unite with the Creator. This is a theme running throughout Japji, as may be seen from the following:

1. Mool Mantar. The Almighty is found Gurprasaad-i/with the guru's grace/guidance.
2. Paurri 1. Question: Kiv koorrai tuttai paal; how does the wall of falsehood break? Answer: Hukam rajaaee chalna Nanak likhiaa naal-i; by conforming to Divine commands brought written with the soul/mind.
3. Paurri 2. Ikna hukmi bakhsees ik hukmi sadaa bhavaaeeah-i; some are bestowed grace – to unite with the Creator, while some are ever in cycles of births and deaths.
4. Paurri 4. Question: Pheyr k-i agai rakheeai jit disai darbar; what offering we should make so that the Almighty is seen? Answer: Amrit veyla sach naau vaddiaaee veechaar; contemplate the eternal Naam/Divine virtues and commands in early morning.

5. Paurri 5. Gaaveeai suneeai man-i rakheeai bhaau, dukh parhar-i sukh ghar-i lai jaaey; we should sing, listen and keep lovingly in mind this ends pain of separation and takes to union with the Creator.
6. Paurri 6. Teerath naavaa jey tis-u bhaava, vin bhaaney k-i naaey karee; I should perform rituals like bathing on pilgrimages if I become pleasing to the Almighty.
7. Paurri 15. Mannai paavai mokhduaar-u; one who obeys Naam gets liberation from vices in life and from rebirth after death; as also entry to the gate of Divine abode, i.e. freedom from temptations and union with the Almighty.
8. Paurri 16. Panch parvaan; those who obey Naam are accepted for union with the Almighty.
9. Paurri 26. Amul bhaaey amula samaah-i; the priceless – those who obey – are liked by, and merge in the Creator.
10. Paurri 32. Eyt raah-u pat-i pavrreeaa charreeai hoey ikees-u; this is the path – of praising and emulating Divine virtues -, to unite with the Creator.
11. Paurri 34. Tithai sohan panch parvaan; there, those who obey Naam are accepted for union by the Almighty.
12. Paurri 37. Sach khandd vasai nirankaar-u; the Formless Supreme Being abides in the realm of the Eternal – if found by Divine grace.
13. Slok/Epilogue. Karmi aapo aapni key neyrrai key door-i; it is by one's own deeds that the creature gets near/merges with, or are kept away from, the Creator.

Paurri 32

ਇਕ ਦੂ ਜੀਭੌ ਲਖ ਹੋਹਿ ਲਖ ਹੋਵਹਿ ਲਖ ਵੀਸ ॥ ਲਖੁ ਲਖੁ ਗੇੜਾ ਆਖੀਅਹਿ ਏ
ਕੁ ਨਾਮੁ ਜਗਦੀਸ ॥ ਏਤੁ ਰਾਹਿ ਪਤਿ ਪਵੜੀਆ ਚੜੀਐ ਹੋਇ ਇਕੀਸ ॥

Ik ḏū jībẖou lakẖ hohi lakẖ hovėh lakẖ vīs. Lakẖ lakẖ geṛā ākẖī▫ahi ek nām jagḏīs. Ėṯ rāhi paṯ pavṛī▫ā cẖaṛī▫ai ho▫e ikīs.

*If (**doo**) from (**ik**) one, the human (**jeebhou**) tongue (**hoh-i**) become a lakh, and from a lakh (**hovah-i**) become (**lakh vees**) twenty lakh; and Naam-u of (**eyk-u**) the One (**jagdees = master of the world**) the Almighty. (**Eyt-u**) these are (**pavrreeaa**) the steps of (**pavrreeaa**) the staircase (**raah-i = the way**) on the path which one needs to (**charreeai**) climb to (**hoey**) become (**ikees**) one/unite (**pat-i**) with, the Creator.*

ਸੁਣਿ ਗਲਾ ਆਕਾਸ ਕੀ ਕੀਟਾ ਆਈ ਰੀਸ ॥ ਨਾਨਕ ਨਦਰੀ ਪਾਈਐ ਕੂੜੀ ਕੂੜੈ ਠੀਸ ॥੩੨॥

Suṇ galā ākās kī kītā ā◌ī rīs. Nānak nadrī pā◌ī◌ai kūṛī kūrhai ṯẖīs. ||32||

*(**Sun-i**) hearing the stories of (**aakaas**) the sky, (**keettaa**) worms – without feathers - also (**aaee = comes**) want (**rees = wishing to copy**) to get there, i.e. hearing of Divine experience, those who do not obey Naam also want to have it. They pretend in many ways, but -*

*Union with the Almighty (**paaeeai**) is attained (**nadree = with sight of grace**) with Divine grace – by complying with Naam; otherwise it is (**koorree**) false (**tthees**) bragging (**koorrai = false one**) of a pretender, says Guru Nanak[1]. 32.*

---

[1] The third Guru gives an analogy:

ਮ: ੩ ॥ ਹੰਸਾ ਵੇਖਿ ਤਰੰਦਿਆ ਬਗਾਂ ਭਿ ਆਯਾ ਚਾਉ ॥ ਡੁਬਿ ਮੁਏ ਬਗ ਬਪੁੜੇ ਸਿਰੁ ਤਲਿ ਉਪਰਿ ਪਾਉ ॥੩॥

Mėhlā 3. Hansā vekẖ ṯarandi◌ā bagāʼn bẖė ā◌yā cẖā◌o. Dub mu◌e bag bapuṛe sir ṯal upar pā◌o. ||3||

Paurri 33

The previous Paurri ended by saying that Union with God/Divine experience comes by Divine grace, which in turn is received by obedience to Divine commands/conformance to Naam. This Paurri uses the expression 'ਨਹ ਜੋਰੁ nah jor-u' or 'ਜੋਰੁ ਨ Jor-u na', both meaning 'without strength/capability', and conveys that the creatures do not have the power/control/capability to achieve what they wish. As will be seen in Paurri 37, this capability comes with Divine grace.

ਆਖਣਿ ਜੋਰੁ ਚੁਪੈ ਨਹ ਜੋਰੁ ॥ ਜੋਰੁ ਨ ਮੰਗਣਿ ਦੇਣਿ ਨ ਜੋਰੁ ॥

Ākẖaṇ jor cẖupai nah jor. Jor na mangaṇ ḏeṇ na jor.

*Neither (**aakhan-i = speaking**) saying what we say nor (**chupai**) keeping quiet, i.e. knowledge or ignorance, is by one's own (**jor-u = power**) capability – it is based on intellect given by the Creator.*

*One cannot (**mangan-i**) ask for peace/union with God by (**jor-u**) force.*

*One does not have (**jor-u**) the ability (**deyn-i**) to give – s/he gives what God gives. 3.*

---

*Prologue by the third Guru. (**Veykh-i**) seeing (**hansa**) the Hans (**tarandiaa**) swimming, (**bagaa-n**) the cranes (**bh-i**) also (**aaya chau**) became eager, to swim.*

*(**Bapurrey**) the poor (**bag**) cranes (**ddub-i muey**) drowned and died in water, with (**sir-u**) head (**tal-i**) down and (**paau**) feet (**upar-i**) up. 3. M: 3, p 585.*

Message: When merit-less persons try to imitate meritorious ones to impress others, they are exposed, and face ignominy.

ਜੋਰੁ ਨ ਜੀਵਣਿ ਮਰਣਿ ਨਹ ਜੋਰੁ ॥ ਜੋਰੁ ਨ ਰਾਜਿ ਮਾਲਿ ਮਨਿ ਸੋਰੁ ॥
Jor na jīvaṇ maraṇ nah jor. Jor na rāj māl man sor.

*It is not in (**jor-u**) power of the creature (**jeevan-i**) to live or (**maran-i**) die.*
*One does not have the ability (**raaj-i = for rule**) to attain high status or acquire wealth – of awareness of Naam; it is only (**sor-u**) noise (**man-i**) mind, i.e. God imparts this awareness by leading to the guru, and following him.*

ਜੋਰੁ ਨ ਸੁਰਤੀ ਗਿਆਨਿ ਵੀਚਾਰਿ ॥ ਜੋਰੁ ਨ ਜੁਗਤੀ ਛੁਟੈ ਸੰਸਾਰੁ ॥
Jor na surṯī gi▫ān vīcẖār. Jor na jugṯī cẖẖutai sansār.

*(**Jor-u**) the ability to have (**giaan-i**) knowledge of (**surtee/Shruti = Vedas**) the scriptures and their (**veechaar-i**) understanding - comes from the guru.*
*It is not by one's own (**jor-u**) power (**jugti = method**) how to (**chhuttai = released**) to give up (**sansaar-u**) the world up, i.e. attain emancipation from rebirth by the self is beyond human capability[1].*

---

[1] Guru Nanak says: ਕਿਆ ਭਵੀਐ ਸਚਿ ਸੂਚਾ ਹੋਇ ॥ ਸਾਚ ਸਬਦ ਬਿਨੁ ਮੁਕਤਿ ਨ ਕੋਇ ॥੧॥ ਰਹਾਉ ॥
Ki▫ā bẖavī▫ai sacẖ sūcẖā ho▫e. Sācẖ sabaḏ bin mukaṯ na ko▫e. ||1|| rahā▫o.

*(**Kiaa**) how can one (**hoey**) become (**soocha = pure**) free of vices and be absorbed (**sach-i**) in the Eternal, (**bhav-i**) by wandering?*
*No, (**mukat-i**) freedom from vices in life and from freedom from rebirth after death – and hence union with the Almighty - is not (**hoey**) obtained (**bin-u**) without following (**sabad = word**) directions of (**saach**) the Eternal. M: 1, p 938 (Sidh Gostt).*
*(**Rahaau**) dwell on this and contemplate*

ਜਿਸੁ ਹਥਿ ਜੋਰੁ ਕਰਿ ਵੇਖੈ ਸੋਇ ॥ ਨਾਨਕ ਉਤਮੁ ਨੀਚੁ ਨ ਕੋਇ ॥੩੩॥

Jis hath jor kar vekẖai so▫e. Nānak uṯam nīcẖ na ko▫e. ||33||

Any one ***(jis-u)*** *who has* ***(jor-u)*** *the power for the above can* ***(kar-i)*** *try and* ***(veykhai)*** *see* ***(soey)*** *that, i.e. only God has that power.*

(Na koey = not any) *no one becomes* ***(utam-u)*** *exalted or* ***(neech-u)*** *low by the self i.e. this applies to all, says Guru Nanak. 33.*

Preface to Paurris 34 to 37

Japji now proceeds to describe the stages of spiritual development that could lead to achievement of the ultimate goal of human life, namely merger with the Divine Spirit from which the soul emanated. These stages or Khandds, meaning divisions/parts/domains/realms, denote the progressive development of state of human mind. The Khandds/realms are as follows:

Paurri 34 - Dharam Khandd: The realm of Divine/cosmic laws, the basis of Divine justice.

Paurri 35 - Giaan Khandd: The realm of knowledge/awareness/understanding Divine laws.

Paurri 36 - Saram Khandd: The realm of endeavour/compliance and transformation.

Paurri 37 Part 1 – Karam Khandd: The realm of Divine grace/enablement.

Paurri 37 Part 2 – Sach-u Khandd: The realm of eternity – union with the Creator.

Paurri 34

ਰਾਤੀ ਰੁਤੀ ਥਿਤੀ ਵਾਰ ॥ ਪਵਣ ਪਾਣੀ ਅਗਨੀ ਪਾਤਾਲ ॥ ਤਿਸੁ ਵਿਚਿ ਧਰਤੀ ਥਾਪਿ ਰਖੀ ਧਰਮ ਸਾਲ ॥

Rāṯī ruṯī thiṯī vār. Pavaṇ pāṇī agnī pāṯāl. Ŧis vicẖ ḏẖarṯī thāp rakẖī ḏẖaram sāl.

*The Creator made cosmic laws by which the sun and moon cause days, (**raati**) nights, (**ruti**) seasons, (**thiti**) phases of the moon, (**vaar**) days of the week.*
*The Creator also created (**pavan**) air, (**paanee**) water, (**agnee**) fire and (**paataal**) lower regions.*
*(**Vich-i**) in (**tis-u**) that set up, - where everything obeys cosmic laws -, the Creator has (**thaap-i = installed, rakhee = kept**) placed (**dharti = earth**) the world as (**saal**) place for (**dharam**) performing duties by the creatures – as laid down for each.*

ਤਿਸੁ ਵਿਚਿ ਜੀਅ ਜੁਗਤਿ ਕੇ ਰੰਗ ॥ ਤਿਨ ਕੇ ਨਾਮ ਅਨੇਕ ਅਨੰਤ ॥
Ŧis vicẖ jī▫a jugaṯ ke rang. Ŧin ke nām anek ananṯ.

*There are (**jeea**) creatures of different (**jugat-i = methods**) roles and (**rang = colors**) types (**vich-i**) in (**tis-u = that**) the world.*
*(**Tin = them, key = of**) their (**naam**) attributes are (**aneyk**) numerous, (**anant = without end**) beyond count, - with their duties and roles and duties prescribed.*

ਕਰਮੀ ਕਰਮੀ ਹੋਇ ਵੀਚਾਰੁ ॥ ਸਚਾ ਆਪਿ ਸਚਾ ਦਰਬਾਰੁ ॥
Karmī karmī ho▫e vīcẖār. Sacẖā āp sacẖā ḏarbār.

*(**Karmee karmee**) deeds of all creature (**hoey = is done,***
***veechaar-u = consideration**) are considered – in light of their duties.*
*(**Aap-i = self**) the Creator is (**sachaa = true**) just and the Divine (**darbaar-u**) court is (**sachaa**) just, i.e. everyone's deeds are evaluated justly, - in the light*

of commands/cosmic laws applicable, and is not arbitrary[1].

ਤਿਥੈ ਸੋਹਹਿ ਪੰਚ ਪਰਵਾਣੁ ॥ ਨਦਰੀ ਕਰਮਿ ਪਵੈ ਨੀਸਾਣੁ ॥
Ŧithai sohan panch̲ parvāṇ. Nad̲rī karam pavai nīsāṇ.

*(**Tithai**) there, in Divine court, (**panch**) those who comply with Divine commands (**sohan-i = look good**) are glorified and (**parvaan-u**) approved. (**Neesaan-u**) the sign (**nadree karam-i**) of Divine grace/approval/acceptance (**pavai = is put**) is marked on them.*

Note: The extended expression ਨਦਰੀ ਕਰਮਿ ਪਵੈ ਨੀਸਾਣੁ meaning 'being marked with sign of grace/approval, is significant. It means those who are blemish-free are so marked and presented before the Almighty marked with honour. The worldly equivalent of this is presentation of 'Siropa' or robe of honour in Gurduaras to those who serve the Guru. The background to this is that in olden days anyone who was to be honoured by a king or queen for virtuous deeds was given a sign before being presented before the king/queen. The fifth Guru describes it thus[2]:

---

[1] Guru Nanak says in Paurri 2 of Aasa Di Vaar: Nanak jeea upaaeykai likh naavai dharam bahaaliaa'othai sacho hi sach nibrrai, chun-i vakh kaddhey jajmaaliaa. The Creator created the creatures to act by Divine commands/laws and gave to Dharam Raaey to watch and judge them in light of the laws. Only those who comply truthfully last, those who do not, are culled. M: 1, p 462.

[2] ਪਹਿਰਿ ਸਿਰਪਾਉ ਸੇਵਕ ਜਨ ਮੇਲੇ ਨਾਨਕ ਪ੍ਰਗਟ ਪਹਾਰੇ ॥ ੨॥੨੯॥੯੩॥
Pahir sirpā▫o sevak jan mele Nānak pargat pahāre. ||2||29||93||

ਕਚ ਪਕਾਈ ਓਥੈ ਪਾਇ ॥ ਨਾਨਕ ਗਇਆ ਜਾਪੈ ਜਾਇ ॥੩੪॥
Kacẖ pakā▫ī othai pā▫e. Nānak ga▫i▫ā jāpai jā▫e. ||34||

*It is (**paaey = received**) told (**othai**) there whether one is (**kach**) unbaked – like earthenware - or (**pakaaee**) baked, i.e. whether one has complied with Divine commands or not. It (**jaapai jaaey**) is known on (**gaiaa = going**) getting there, when record of deeds is shown, says Guru Nanak. 34.*

Paurri 35

In order to carry out one's duties it is necessary to understand them. Paurri 35, which is about the Realm of Knowledge, or Giaan Khandd, gives this understanding. It first starts by saying:

ਧਰਮ ਖੰਡ ਕਾ ਏਹੋ ਧਰਮੁ ॥ ਗਿਆਨ ਖੰਡ ਕਾ ਆਖਹੁ ਕਰਮੁ ॥
Ḏẖaram kẖand kā eho ḏẖaram. Gi▫ān kẖand kā ākẖhu karam.

*(**Eyho**) this is (**dharam-u**) the role of (**khandd**) the realm of (**dharam**) dutifulness – the creatures are to conform to, and are judged, in light of Divine commands/laws/duties.*
*Let us now (**aakhahu = say**) understand (**karam-u = doing**) the role of (**khanndd**) the realm of (**giaan**) knowledge/understanding about Divine commands.*

Note: The above means that one instinctively obeys commands when one understands the environment. It

---

*Such a (**jan**) person/soul then (**pahir-i**) wears (**sirpaau**) the robe of honour, i.e. honourably (**meyley**) finds the Almighty, and is (**pargatt = manifest**) respected in (**pahaarey = expanse**) in the world – by all. 2. 29. 93. M: 5, p 631.*

is like the first thing taught in military is drill, where the recruits march to orders without going anywhere.

ਕੇਤੇ ਪਵਣ ਪਾਣੀ ਵੈਸੰਤਰ ਕੇਤੇ ਕਾਨ ਮਹੇਸ ॥ ਕੇਤੇ ਬਰਮੇ ਘਾੜਤਿ ਘੜੀਅਹਿ ਰੂਪ ਰੰਗ ਕੇ ਵੇਸ ॥ ਕੇਤੀਆ ਕਰਮ ਭੂਮੀ ਮੇਰ ਕੇਤੇ ਕੇਤੇ ਧੂ ਉਪਦੇਸ ॥
Keṯe pavaṇ pāṇī vaisanṯar keṯe kān mahes. Keṯe barme gẖāṛaṯ gẖaṛī▫ahi rūp rang ke ves. Keṯī▫ā karam bẖūmī mer keṯe keṯe ḏẖū upḏes.

*There are (**keytey = so many**) numerous (**pavan = air**) gases, (**paanee = water**) liquids and (**vaisantar = fires**) forms of energy like light and heat – of which the creation is comprised; as also numerous (**kaan = Krishnas**) incarnations of Vishnu, and Mahesh - who is also called Shankar, Mahadev, or Shiva – and worshipped by people.*
*There are (**ketey = so many**) numerous (**barmey**) Brahmas with their creations of many (**roop**) forms, (**rang = colors**) hues and (**veys = attire**) types.*
*There are numerous (**bhoomee = land**) fields/types of roles the creatures (**karam**) perform like Bhagat Dhru went to (**meyr**) the Sumeyr mountain and numerous guides - like the mythological Narada.*

Message: All the above are created by, and represent play of, the Creator.
ਕੇਤੇ ਇੰਦ ਚੰਦ ਸੂਰ ਕੇਤੇ ਕੇਤੇ ਮੰਡਲ ਦੇਸ ॥ ਕੇਤੇ ਸਿਧ ਬੁਧ ਨਾਥ ਕੇਤੇ ਕੇਤੇ ਦੇਵੀ ਵੇਸ ॥
Keṯe inḏ cẖanḏ sūr keṯe keṯe mandal ḏes. Keṯe siḏẖ buḏẖ nāth keṯe keṯe ḏevī ves.

*There are numerous (**ind**) Indra/skies, numerous (**chand**) moons and (**soor**) suns; numerous galaxies and (**deys = countries**) planets.*
*There are numerous (**sidh**) saints, (**budh**) Buddhas, (**naath**) Naath Yogis and numerous (**veys = garbs**)*

*forms of (**deyvi**) the goddesses – who are worshipped, but themselves obey the Creator.*

It is interesting to note that unlike one each of the gods like Brahma, Vishnu and Mahesh in the Hindu belief, Guru Nanak says there are many of them. This confirms that the adjective 'One' applies only to the Creator as described in the Mool Mantar.

ਕੇਤੇ ਦੇਵ ਦਾਨਵ ਮੁਨਿ ਕੇਤੇ ਕੇਤੇ ਰਤਨ ਸਮੁੰਦ ॥ ਕੇਤੀਆ ਖਾਣੀ ਕੇਤੀਆ ਬਾਣੀ ਕੇਤੇ ਪਾਤ ਨਰਿੰਦ ॥ ਕੇਤੀਆ ਸੁਰਤੀ ਸੇਵਕ ਕੇਤੇ ਨਾਨਕ ਅੰਤੁ ਨ ਅੰਤੁ ॥੩੫॥
Keṯe ḏev ḏānav mun keṯe keṯe raṯan samunḏ. Keṯī▫ā kẖāṇī keṯī▫ā baṇī keṯe pāṯ narinḏ. Keṯī▫ā surṯī sevak keṯe Nānak anṯ na anṯ. ||35||

*There are (**keytey**) numerous (**deyv**) gods – objects of worship -, (**daanav**) demons – causes of distraction -, (**mun-i**) silent sages and (**ratan**) the jewels in (**samund**) the sea.*
*There are (**keyteeaa**) numerous (**khaanee**) ways the creatures are born – from egg, womb, perspiration (heat and humidity) and from soil, with (**keyteeaa**) numerous (**baanee/banat = construction**) types of bodies; there are (**keytey**) numerous kings/queens – they are all subject to Divine commands.*
*There are numerous (**surtee/Shruti = Vedas**) scriptures which ask to obey the Almighty, and their (**seyvak = servants**) followers/readers; there is (**na**) no (**ant-u = end**) count of types of creation owing allegiance to (**na = no, ant-u = limit**) the Infinite. 35.*

Note: Reference to the jewels in the sea above is with respect to Hindu mythology that when the gods churned the ocean 14 jewels came out. It was detailed in Paurri 27. As stated there, the Sikh concept of churning the sea refers to churning/reflecting in the mind to recognise God within.

Paurri 36.

ਗਿਆਨ ਖੰਡ ਮਹਿ ਗਿਆਨੁ ਪਰਚੰਡੁ ॥ ਤਿਥੈ ਨਾਦ ਬਿਨੋਦ ਕੋਡ ਅਨੰਦੁ ॥

Gi▫ān kẖand mėh gi▫ān parcẖand. Ŧithai nāḏ binoḏ kod anand.

*(**Giaan-u**) awareness - of Naam/Divine virtues and commands - (**parchadd-u = mighty**) is dominant in Giaan Khandd, the realm of knowledge, i.e. one learns to act by Naam, dispel other ideas, shun transgressions and there is no anxiety. Hence (**tithai**) there, (**mah-i**) in Giaan Khandd one enjoys (**anand-u**) bliss/joy of (**kodd**) crores of (**naad**) music, (**binod**) merry-making, and one makes effort to find the Master, states Paurri 36*[1].

Note: Once again as in Paurri 35, inclusion of these two lines before describing Saram Khandd shows that the latter stage comes after Giaan Khandd.

Also, the second line above may be compared with the last line of each of Pauris 8 to 11 on the subject of 'Suniai' or 'listening, - which is a means of obtaining knowledge -, saying that with this the devotees feel joy.

---

[1] This is restatement of the two lines of Paurris 8-11 about (suniai/listening learning.

ਨਾਨਕ ਭਗਤਾ ਸਦਾ ਵਿਗਾਸੁ ॥ ਸੁਣਿਐ ਦੂਖ ਪਾਪ ਕਾ ਨਾਸੁ ॥

Nānak bẖagṯā saḏā vigās. Suṇi▫ai ḏūkẖ pāp kā nās.

*Says Guru Nanak: (**Bhagta**) the devotees are (**sadaa**) ever (**vigaas-u = blossom**) joyful;*
*Because (**dookh**) faults and (**paap**) transgressions (**naas-u = destruction**) end (**suniai**) by listening/obeying, and there is no fear, apprehension of consequences or sense of guilt.*

Saram Khandd is the realm of endeavour to transform the self. The mind, enlightened by Giaan/awareness of Naam, moulds itself by complying with Naam; it is sincere obedience to Divine commands. This is how.

ਸਰਮ ਖੰਡ ਕੀ ਬਾਣੀ ਰੂਪੁ ॥ ਤਿਥੈ ਘਾੜਤਿ ਘੜੀਐ ਬਹੁਤੁ ਅਨੂਪੁ ॥
Saram kẖand kī baṇī rūp. Ŧithai gẖāṛaṯ gẖaṛī▫ai bahuṯ anūp.

*(**Baani/bantar**) construction/state of (**khandd**) the realm of (**saram**) effort/obedience is (**roop-u**) beauty.*
*(**Tithai**) there, (**ghaarrat-i = sculpture**) the mind (**gharreeai**) is sculpted/transformed to (**bahut-u**) highly (**anoop-u**) incomparable beauty, i.e. the mind is different from ordinary minds which succumb to temptations/other ideas, - and the most sublime state of freedom from temptations is attained.*

ਤਾ ਕੀਆ ਗਲਾ ਕਥੀਆ ਨਾ ਜਾਹਿ ॥ ਜੇ ਕੋ ਕਹੈ ਪਿਛੈ ਪਛੁਤਾਇ ॥
Ŧā kī▫ā galā kathī▫ā nā jāhi. Je ko kahai picẖẖai pacẖẖuṯā▫e.

*(**Galaa = things**) the state (**ki**) of (**ta**) that mind (**na jaaey**) cannot be (**katheeaa**) stated; (**jey**) if (**ko**) someone (**kahai = says**) describes, s/he (**pachhutaaey**) repents (**pichhai**) later – for not being able to do justice.*

Note: This is re-statement of Paurri 12 which uses almost the
same words in respect of Ma'nney or obedience:

ਮੰਨੇ ਕੀ ਗਤਿ ਕਹੀ ਨ ਜਾਇ ॥ ਜੇ ਕੋ ਕਹੈ ਪਿਛੈ ਪਛੁਤਾਇ ॥

Manne kī gaṯ kahī na jā▫e. Je ko kahai picẖẖai pacẖẖuṯā▫e.

*(**Gat-i = state**) the exalted state of – freedom from temptations that is attained by - (**manney**) accepting/obeying Naam (**na jaaey**) cannot be (**kahee**) told – it can only be experienced.*
*(**Jey**) if (**ko**) someone (**kahai**) says, (**pachhutaaey**) repents (**pichhai**) later, i.e. realizes that s/he has not been able to correctly describe it.*

How is the mind shaped/transformed?

ਤਿਥੈ ਘੜੀਐ ਸੁਰਤਿ ਮਤਿ ਮਨਿ ਬੁਧਿ ॥ ਤਿਥੈ ਘੜੀਐ ਸੁਰਾ ਸਿਧਾ ਕੀ ਸੁਧਿ ॥੩੬॥
Ŧithai gẖaṛī▫ai suraṯ maṯ man buḏẖ. Ŧithai gẖaṛī▫ai surā siḏẖā kī suḏẖ. ||36||

*(**Tithai**) there, (**surat-i**) consciousness, (**mat-i**) thinking faculty (**man-i**) of the mind and (**budh-i**) understanding (**gharreeai**) are carved/shaped.*
*(**Tithai**) there, one (**gharreeai**) shapes (**sudh-i**) awareness like that of (**suraa**) gods and (**sidhaa**) accomplished saints, i.e. those who experience God's presence. 36.*

Message: One lives with focus on obedience to the Almighty, does not get distracted.

Note: We are in the process of discussing the five Khandds in Japji. The first three namely Dharam Khandd, the Realm of Duty, Giaan Khandd the Realm of Knowledge and Saram Khandd the Realm of effort were sequentially discussed in Paurris 34 to 36. These three lie in human domain in that they are to be done by the humans with the help of the guru. The next two are in hands of the Divine.

Paurri 37

Paurri 37 discusses the fourth and fifth Khandds namely Karam Khandd the Realm of Divine Grace and Sach Khandd the realm of truthfulness. Both these lie in the domain of the Divine, the second being the consequence of the first, and understandably discussed together.

Note: Paurri 33 stated that the human being does not have ਜੋਰੁ (Jor-u) meaning strength or ability for numerous things. Paurri 37 says that ability can come by Divine grace

ਕਰਮ ਖੰਡ ਕੀ ਬਾਣੀ ਜੋਰੁ ॥ ਤਿਥੈ ਹੋਰੁ ਨ ਕੋਈ ਹੋਰੁ ॥

Karam kẖand kī baṇī jor. Ŧithai hor na ko▫ī hor.

***(Baanee = construction/shape)** the state of **(khandd)** the realm/the recipient of **(karam)** Divine grace is **(jor-u)** strength – ability to overcome temptations and focus on Naam.*
***(Tithai)** there – in this state of the mind –, there is **(na koee = not any)** none **(hor-u)** else that one looks to, and no **(hor-u)** other thought comes to mind.*

ਤਿਥੈ ਜੋਧ ਮਹਾਬਲ ਸੂਰ ॥ ਤਿਨ ਮਹਿ ਰਾਮੁ ਰਹਿਆ ਭਰਪੂਰ ॥

Ŧithai joḏẖ mahābal sūr. Ŧin mėh rām rahi▫ā bẖarpūr.

*There are **(mahabal)** very mighty **(jodh)** warriors and **(soor)** fighters **(tithai)** there, i.e. they have the strength because of Divine grace. It conveys that Divine grace gives ordinary persons the ability to overcome temptations in life. Only **(raam-u)** the*

*Almighty (**rahiaa**) remains (**bharpoor**) fully filling their minds – with no room for anything else.*

ਤਿਥੈ ਸੀਤੋ ਸੀਤਾ ਮਹਿਮਾ ਮਾਹਿ ॥ ਤਾ ਕੇ ਰੂਪ ਨ ਕਥਨੇ ਜਾਹਿ ॥

Ŧithai sīṯo sīṯā mahimā māhi. Ŧā ke rūp na kathne jāhi.

*In this state, the creatures are (**seeto seeta = stitched and stitched**) woven (**maah-i**) in (**mahimaa**) praise of the Almighty, i.e. engrossed in compliance of Naam.*

*(**Key = of, ta = them**) their (**roop = beauty**) exalted states (**na jaah-i**) cannot (**kathey**) be described.* (Note: This may be linked to "tithai ghaarrat-i gharreeai bahut-u annoop – there shape of incomparable beauty is carved, in Paurri 36).

ਨਾ ਓਹਿ ਮਰਹਿ ਨ ਠਾਗੇ ਜਾਹਿ ॥ ਜਿਨ ਕੈ ਰਾਮੁ ਵਸੈ ਮਨ ਮਾਹਿ ॥

Nā ohi marėh na ṯẖāge jāhi. Jin kai rām vasai man māhi.

*(**Oh-i**) they neither (**marah-i = die**) succumb to temptations nor (**tthaagey jaah-i = are cheated**) deluded by other ideas to go astray. They are those (**maah-i**) in (**kai = of, jin = whom**) whose (**man**) minds (**raam-u**) the Almighty (**vasai**) abides – and other ideas dispelled.*

ਤਿਥੈ ਭਗਤ ਵਸਹਿ ਕੇ ਲੋਅ ॥ ਕਰਹਿ ਅਨੰਦੁ ਸਚਾ ਮਨਿ ਸੋਇ ॥

Ŧithai bẖagaṯ vasėh ke lo▫a. Karahi anand sacẖā man so▫e.

*(**Tithai**) there are found (**loa**) habitats (**vasah-i**) for stay (**key**) of (**bhagat**) the devotees; they (**karah-i**) enjoy (**anand-u**) bliss with (**soey = that one**) the*

*Almighty (**man-i**) in mind – free from temptations -, this is Karam Khandd, the realm of Divine grace.*

Karam Khand therefore is the state of mind where one realizes that s/he does not do anything; everything is attributed to the Creator. This Divine grace enables one to enter the abode of the Eternal Lord, or Sach Khandd, the realm of truthfulness, described in the second part of Paurri 37:
Such people or devotees receive the power to overcome impediments and proceed to be with God. They are able to

have vision of the formless Creator - seeing God within:

Note: Japji has earlier mentioned talked of "ਮੋਖ ਦੁਆਰ" Mokh-
u Duaar, the emancipation from temptations and entry to (gate) abode of the Almighty, obviating cycles of births and deaths thrice earlier. Paurri 2 said "Ikna hukmee bakhsees, ik hukmee sadaa bhaaveeah-i" – some receive Bakhsees/Divine grace to merge with God, while some ever remain in cycles of births and deaths. Paurri 4 said "karmee aavai kaprra nadree mokh duaar" human birth is obtained by good deeds – here 'karmi' means by deeds – and freedom from temptations and entry to/union with the Creator - comes 'nadree' by Divine grace. Paurri 15 said "mannai paavai mokh duaar-u" freedom from temptations and union with the Almighty obviating further births and deaths. This is what reaching Sach Khandd implies.

Paurri 37 Part 2

ਸਚ ਖੰਡਿ ਵਸੈ ਨਿਰੰਕਾਰੁ ॥ ਕਰਿ ਕਰਿ ਵੇਖੈ ਨਦਰਿ ਨਿਹਾਲ ॥

Sach khand vasai nirankār. Kar kar vekhai nadar nihāl.

*(**Nirankaar-u**) the Formless Almighty (**vasai**) abides in (**khandd-i**) in the realm of (**sach**) truthfulness – in conforming to Naam. The Almighty (**kar-i kar-i**) having created the creatures, (**veykhai**) looks (**nadar-i**) sight of grace (**nihaal**) to bestow happiness, i.e. fulfils yearning for union of those who qualify to enter the Sach Khandd.*

ਤਿਥੈ ਖੰਡ ਮੰਡਲ ਵਰਭੰਡ ॥ ਜੇ ਕੋ ਕਥੈ ਤ ਅੰਤ ਨ ਅੰਤ ॥

Ŧithai kẖand mandal varbẖand. Je ko kathai ṯa anṯ na anṯ.

*All (**khandd**) planets, (**manddal**) galaxies and the whole (**varbhandd**) universe are covered (**tithai**) there – in the Almighty's domain.*

*(**Jey**) if (**ko**) someone (**kathai**) tries to describe the creation (**ta**) then s/he realises there is no (**ant**) limit to (**ant**) the expanse.*

ਤਿਥੈ ਲੋਅ ਲੋਅ ਆਕਾਰ ॥ ਜਿਵ ਜਿਵ ਹੁਕਮੁ ਤਿਵੈ ਤਿਵ ਕਾਰ ॥

Ŧithai lo▫a lo▫a ākār. Jiv jiv hukam ṯivai ṯiv kār.

*(**Loa loa = various worlds**) all planets and habitats and (**aakaar = physical form**) of the creation are (**tithai**) there in Divine domain.*

*(**Jiv jiv**) as is (**hukam-u = order**) the law for each type (**tivai tiv = similar**) so is (**kaar**) compliance, i.e. only those who comply with Divine commands attain the state of Sach Khandd.*

ਵੇਖੈ ਵਿਗਸੈ ਕਰਿ ਵੀਚਾਰੁ ॥ ਨਾਨਕ ਕਥਨਾ ਕਰੜਾ ਸਾਰੁ ॥੩੭॥

vekẖai vigsai kar vīcẖār. Nānak kathnā karṛā sār. ||37||

*The Almighty (**vigsai**) is happy as IT (**veykhai**) sees and (**kar-i = doing, veechaar-u = consideration**) considers their deeds.*
*(**Kathna**) describing the state of those in Sach Khandd is (**kararra**) hard like (**saar**) iron/steel, says Guru Nanak. 37.*

Paurri 38

Paurris 34-37 described the stages in reaching the state of Sach Khandd. This is not a one-time occurrence, except final union of the soul on death of the body. One is subject to spells of temptations, which cause one to waver. Paurri 38 describes how the state of Sach Khandd may be maintained. This involves getting rid of impurities, make the mind responsive to the guru's teachings and keep it as has been done in Paurris 34-37.

Paurri 38 uses the manual process of making gold ornaments as metaphor to understand this. The goldsmith purifies gold by boiling it in a crucible on a furnace heated by burning charcoal to rid it of impurities. Bellows/blower intensifies the fire of the charcoal. The liquid gold keeps boiling until the impurities in it are burned. When it stops boiling, it is poured into a mould for rough shape and then placed on an anvil and given final form by the goldsmith using tools. This process covers four of the five Khandds – less Sach Khandd. This is how:

ਜਤੁ ਪਾਹਾਰਾ ਧੀਰਜੁ ਸੁਨਿਆਰੁ ॥

Jaṯ pāhārā ḏẖīraj suni▫ār.

*(**Jat-u = celibacy**) self-discipline is (**paahaara**) the workshop and (**suniaar-u**) the goldsmith/human being, the epitome of (**dheeraj-u = patience**) perseverance, i.e. one is to perform one's duties*

diligently in face of impediments/distractions. This is dutifulness, Dharam Khandd.

ਅਹਰਣਿ ਮਤਿ ਵੇਦੁ ਹਥੀਆਰੁ ॥

Ahraṇ maṯ veḏ hathīoār.

*(**Mat-i**) thinking faculty is placed (**ahran-i**) on the anvil and shaped with (**veyd-u = spiritual knowledge**) awareness of Naam as (**hatheear-u**) the tool, i.e. the mind should be responsive to the guru's teachings.* This is knowledge, Giaan Khandd.

ਭਉ ਖਲਾ ਅਗਨਿ ਤਪ ਤਾਉ ॥ ਭਾਂਡਾ ਭਾਉ ਅੰਮ੍ਰਿਤੁ ਤਿਤੁ ਢਾਲਿ ॥ ਘੜੀਐ ਸਬਦੁ ਸਚੀ ਟਕਸਾਲ ॥

Bẖao khalā agan ṯap ṯāo. Bẖāʼndā bẖāo amriṯ ṯiṯ dẖāl. Gẖaṛīoai sabaḏ sacẖī taksāl.

*(**Bhau = fear**) respect/obedience of the Almighty is (**khalaa**) the bellows/blower to feed the fire and (**tap = austerities**) bearing hardships is (**taau**) the heat, i.e. one should sacrifice one's comforts to sincerely obey Divine commands.*
*(**Bhaau = love**) devoted mind is (**bha'ndda = vessel**) the mould and in (**tit-u**) that molten (**amrit**) gold (**ddhaal-i**) is poured to cast, i.e. one lovingly receive Naam in the devoted mind.*
*This is (**sachi**) the true (**taksaal**) mint where life (**gharreeai**) is carved/shaped according to (**sabad-u = Divine word**) Divine commands/Naam.* This is Saram Khandd.

ਜਿਨ ਕਉ ਨਦਰਿ ਕਰਮੁ ਤਿਨ ਕਾਰ ॥

Jin kao naḏar karam ṯin kār.

*This (**kaar**) work/way of life is of (**tin**) those (**kau**) on (**jin**) whom (**nadar-i**) sight of (**karam-u**) Divine grace is bestowed.* This is Divine grace, Karam Khandd.

ਨਾਨਕ ਨਦਰੀ ਨਦਰਿ ਨਿਹਾਲ ॥੩੮॥

Nānak nadrī nadar nihāl. ||38||
*They are (**nihaal**) happy/blessed with (**nadar-i**) grace of (**nadri = bestower**) of the Almighty, says Guru Nanak.* This is Sach Khandd. *38.*

The five khands thus are the final stages of the journey which starts with Gurparsad-i (knowing through Guru's grace), continues with living according to Hukam and finally receiving Divine grace leading to being one with the Creator.

Slok (epilogue).

ਪਵਣੁ ਗੁਰੂ ਪਾਣੀ ਪਿਤਾ ਮਾਤਾ ਧਰਤਿ ਮਹਤੁ ॥ ਦਿਵਸੁ ਰਾਤਿ ਦੁਇ ਦਾਈ ਦਾਇਆ ਖੇਲੈ ਸਗਲ ਜਗਤੁ ॥

Salok. Pavaṇ gurū pāṇī piṯā māṯā ḏẖaraṯ mahaṯ. Ḏivas rāṯ ḏuᵒe ḏāᵒī ḏāᵒiᵒā kẖelai sagal jagaṯ.

*Human birth takes place with (**paanee = water**) semen of (**pitaa**) father and egg of (**maataa**) the mother – like a plant grows in (dharat-i) soil with seed and water. It has (**mahat-u/Mahatav**) importance, being the opportunity to live by Naam and attain union with the Creator*[1]. *(Note: The word ਮਹਤੁ Mahat-*

[1] Kabir Ji says:

ਗਉੜੀ ॥ ਪਾਨੀ ਮੈਲਾ ਮਾਟੀ ਗੋਰੀ ॥ ਇਸ ਮਾਟੀ ਕੀ ਪੁਤਰੀ ਜੋਰੀ ॥੧॥

Gaᵒoṛī. Pānī mailā mātī gorī. Is mātī kī puṯrī jorī. ||1||

*Gaurri. With (**maila = dirty**) the turbid (**paani**) water/father's semen and egg in (**maatti = soil**) uterous of (**gori**) the female,* *u having an Aunkarr to ੳ at the end indicates masculine reference, so cannot apply to Maata/mother or earth being female according to Gurbani grammar); **(pavan-u)** the word/Divine commands are **(guru)** the guru, the controller of life/body.*

*The sun causes the **(duey)** the two phenomena of **(raat-i)** night acting as **(daaee)** female nanny– meant for rest, and **(divas-u)** day as **(daaiaa)** male nanny – meant for activities; **(sagal)** the whole **(jagat-u)** world, **(kheylai)** plays, i.e. the creatures conform to these phenomena*[1]*.*

---

*(**putri = puppet**) the body is (**jori**) formed. 1. Kabir, p 336.*

[1] Guru Nanak also says:
ਪਉਣੁ ਗੁਰੁ ਪਾਣੀ ਪਿਤ ਜਾਤਾ ॥ ਉਦਰ ਸੰਜੋਗੀ ਧਰਤੀ ਮਾਤਾ ॥ ਰੈਣਿ ਦਿਨਸੁ ਦੁਇ ਦਾਈ ਦਾਇਆ ਜਗੁ ਖੇਲੈ ਖੇਲਾਈ ਹੇ ॥੧੦॥ Pa▫uṇ gurū pāṇī piṯ jāṯā. Uḏar sanjogī ḏẖarṯī māṯā. Raiṇ ḏinas ḏu▫e ḏā▫ī ḏā▫i▫ā jag kẖelai kẖelā▫ī he. ||10||

*(**Paun-u = air**) the soul (**jaataa = known**) is considered the guru and (**paani**) water/semen (**pit/pitaa**) the father; (**Udar = abdomen**) uterus of (**maataa**) the mother which (**sanjogi**) brings together – the male semen and female egg - is like (**dharti**) the earth with, i.e. the fetus is formed in the womb like plants grow in the soil.*

*(**Duey = two**) both (**rain-i**) night and (**dinas-u**) day are (**daaee**) female nanny and (**daaiaa**) male nanny respectively; (**jag-u = world**) the creature (**kheylai**) plays as it is (**kheylaaee**) caused to play, i.e. phenomena of day and night guide human activities. 10. M: 1, p 1021.*

Note: As may be seen, these verses refer to a human being – being born and activities guided by the phenomena of day and night. So just saying water is father and earth as mother, as is the usual translation, does not convey anything.

ਚੰਗਿਆਈਆ ਬੁਰਿਆਈਆ ਵਾਚੈ ਧਰਮੁ ਹਦੂਰਿ ॥ ਕਰਮੀ ਆਪੋ ਆਪਣੀ ਕੇ ਨੇੜੈ ਕੇ ਦੂਰਿ ॥

Chang▫ā▫ī▫ā buri▫ā▫ī▫ā vācẖai ḏẖaram haḏūr. Karmī āpo āpṇī ke neṛai ke ḏūr.

*(**Dharam-u**) Dharam Rai the metaphoric judge of Divine court (**vaachai = says**) narrates (**changiaaeeaa**) merits or obedience and (**buriaaeeaa**) demerits or transgressions - of the creature (**hadoor-i**) before the Almighty.*

*Depending on (**karmi = doings**) deeds (**aapo aapni = own of each**) everyone (**ko**) some – those who conform to*

*Naam – go (**neyrrai**) near/unite with the Almighty while (**ko**) some – the transgressors -, are kept (**door-i**) away.*

ਜਿਨੀ ਨਾਮੁ ਧਿਆਇਆ ਗਏ ਮਸਕਤਿ ਘਾਲਿ ॥ਨਾਨਕ ਤੇ ਮੁਖ ਉਜਲੇ ਕੇਤੀ ਛੁਟੀ ਨਾਲਿ ॥੧॥

Jinī nām ḏẖi▫ā▫i▫ā ga▫e maskaṯ gẖāl. Nānak ṯe mukẖ ujle keṯī cẖẖutī nāl. ||1||

*(**Jini**) those (**dhiaaiaa**) pay attention/conform to (**naam-u**) Naam, they (**gaey**) depart from the world (**ghaal-i**) having put in (**masakat-i**) effort – acted as directed by the Almighty.*

*(**Tey**) those (**mukh**) faces are (**ujley**) radiant, i.e. those souls are found without faults and united with the Almighty; (**ketey**) numerous others (**naal-i = with**) in their company (**chhuttee = freed**) are not*

detained by Divine justice and unite, says Guru Nanak. 1.

Note: Equation of Naam/Divine commands to cosmic laws withstands scrutiny since Paurri 34 said the earth has been nominated to perform duties in the setup of nights, days, seasons, air and water, which comply cosmic laws. Also, the Slok itself says human activities are governed by the natural phenomena of nights and days.

Note: God is present within the body as conscience/the motivator, and as controller of the creation according to natural laws outside. The ability of the soul to unite with the Almighty on death is preceded by satisfying the conscience with our thoughts deeds. This is the same as conformance to Naam/cosmic laws or natural laws for union with the Almighty on death. Spiritual and secular lives cannot be separated.

Acknowledgements

The author thankfully acknowledges the following.

1. Having referered to:

    - Shabdarath Sri Guru Granth Sahib Ji by Shromni Gurduara Parbandhak committee.
    - Mahan Kosh by Bhai Kahn Singh Nabha.
    - Santhya Sri Guru Granth Sahib by Dr Vir Singh.
    - Sri Guru Granth Sahib Darpan by Prof Sahib Singh.
    - Fareed Kote Wala Teeka

2. Permission by Dr Kulbir Thind to use the transliteration given in Srigranth.org.
3. Help by my nephew Dr Harpreet Singh, Boston, USA for technical guidance and execution.
4. S. Gurmukh Singh of United Kingdom for continued encouragement and suggestions.

Made in the USA
Las Vegas, NV
11 July 2023

74522373R00098